Essential Guide to the Library IBM PC

Volume 14
The Operating System:
PC-DOS

The Essential Guide to the Library IBM PC

Series Editor: Nancy Melin Nelson
Series ISBN 0–88736–080–7

Additional volumes in preparation

Essential Guide to the Library IBM PC

Volume 14
The Operating System: PC-DOS

by
Karl Beiser

Meckler

Westport • London

Library of Congress Cataloging-in-Publication Data

(Revised for vol. 14)

Essential guide to the library IBM PC.

Includes bibliographies and indexes.
Contents: v.1. The hardware, set-up and expansion /
Nancy Jean Melin—[etc.]—v. 8. Library applications
of optical disk and CD-ROM technology / by Nancy Melin
Nelson— —v. 14. The operating system, PC-DOS /
by Karl Beiser.
1. Libraries—Automation. 2. Microcomputers—Library
applications. 3. IBM Personal Computer—Programming.
I. Nelson, Nancy Melin.
Z678.9.E86 1985   025.3'028'5   85–10535
ISBN 0–88736–080–7 (pbk. : set)
ISBN 0–88736–033–5 (pbk. : v. 1)
ISBN 0–88736–350–4 (pbk. : v. 14)

British Library Cataloguing in Publication Data

Beiser, Karl
    Essential guide to the library IBM PC.
    Vol. 14: The operating system PC-DOS
    1. Libraries. Applications of IBM PC microcomputer
    systems
    1. Title
    025'.0028'5

    ISBN 0–88736–350–4

Meckler Corporation, 11 Ferry Lane West, Westport, CT 06880.
Meckler Ltd., Grosvenor Gardens House, Grosvenor Gardens,
London SW1W OBS, U.K.

Printed on acid-free paper.
Printed in the United States of America.

To Martha, without whose love and support
most things would not be possible,
and to Natalie and Maggie who make it all worthwhile.

CONTENTS

INTRODUCTION

IBM-compatible computers are everywhere. They are the workhorses of a wide range of microcomputer software applications in libraries. Unfortunately, effective use of these compatibles is not transparently easy to learn. This book will help you grasp the fundamentals and get "up and running" fast.

Novices and veteran computer users—whether they seek an introduction to the learning process or a reference work to turn to when they require quick, clear explanations of more advanced DOS commands and features—will find helpful material here.

Starting From the Beginning

The hardest thing for most new users of DOS (disk operating system) is figuring out where to start. While it may be true that "it's all in the manual," most manuals require you to know that something exists before you can look it up. Here, we start at the beginning. The essential concepts and commands you will need to hit the ground running are segregated and spotlighted. The less-used facilities of DOS are readily recognized as of lesser initial importance by the fact that they are treated later. Most computer users will find the majority of their initial needs addressed in the early chapters. As your experience and your needs grow, you will be able to proceed at a measured pace through subsequent sections.

Please keep in mind that this presentation, like any introduction to a computer topic, is necessarily an exercise in controlled simplification. The most important points are emphasized, while complicating and generally irrelevant details are treated lightly. Examples of usage always start out with the most simple and most frequent applications and progress to the more esoteric.

While this is an introduction to a technical subject, it is also a personally guided tour. You should not be surprised, therefore, to find some opinion and speculation along with the technicalities of using DOS.

What is DOS?

DOS is a special set of computer-readable instructions called an "operating system." The operating system serves as the intermediary between applications software designed for a wide range of computer systems and the specific computer on which that applications software is running.

Saving information to a disk drive may be initiated from within WordPerfect, for instance, but the mechanics of sticking sequences of alphanumeric characters in particular sectors and tracks of a disk storage device—and finding them later—are handled by facilities built into DOS. Interaction between the keyboard, the display, computer memory, printer port, communications port, and other components of the computer system is managed and coordinated by the operating system. The effect is to free applications programmers from having to reinvent the wheel to handle the structured underpinnings of computer usage.

Without DOS, no other software will run. Thus, DOS must somehow be loaded into the computer's random-access memory before anything else. IBM-compatible computers automatically retrieve DOS from a disk drive—if it is stored there—when the computer is turned on. Only after DOS is running can other programs be loaded and run.

DOS comes in two major varieties: IBM markets DOS as "DOS," though it is commonly referred to as PC-DOS; Microsoft's equivalent is called MS-DOS. Microsoft and IBM have worked together on the development of DOS since introduction of the IBM Personal Computer in 1981. Through version 3.2, Microsoft did the major portion of development work and licensed the result to IBM; the process has reversed with versions 3.3 and 4.0. MS-DOS is sold to manufacturers of IBM compatibles who package it with their computer systems. Some manufacturers customize MS-DOS to take fuller advantage of particular features not found on all machines. Others make no changes at all. You can also buy a generic version of MS-DOS from some mail-order suppliers. Highly compatible computer systems should run equally well with PC-DOS and MS-DOS. However, the introduction of IBM's DOS 4.0 has presented new sources of incompatibility such that some clones will not run with it as of this writing.

The Evolution of DOS

DOS has changed considerably since version 1.0 was shipped with IBM's PC in 1981. Version 1.1 fixed some bugs in the original version and added several new features. With the introduction of the IBM PC/XT, a system with a (then) enormous 10 megabytes (MB) of hard disk storage, came the need for support of large magnetic disk storage devices. Version 2.0, followed quickly by 2.1, met the needs of hard disk users.

The growing importance of local-area networks (LANs) and the move to the IBM PC/AT brought forth version 3.0. Better support for networks and for newer disk formats resulted in 3.1, 3.2, and 3.3. Along the way, a miscellany of other useful new commands and overdue enhancements to older commands was added.

IBM introduced version 4.0 of DOS in July 1988. Its most obvious in-
novation is the inclusion of a menu-based user interface designed to make
DOS easier to learn and use. The 32-MB limit on the size of a single logical
disk drive was removed and support for use of expanded memory was improved.

Learning DOS

DOS is to using a computer what wiring is to living in a house—though you
can't get along without knowing how to use outlets and switches and replace
a fuse if it blows, you don't need to know how to rewire the master service
panel. Indeed, unless you are an electrician, the entire subject probably holds
little inherent interest for you.

Don't think of DOS mastery as a first skill. You don't need to learn all
about DOS before going on to such fun stuff as mastering a word-processing
program that makes your work suddenly much, much easier. You will learn
best and use your time most wisely if you concentrate at first on the bare essentials. They are easily and quickly learned. From there, learn only as many
additional commands and concepts as your needs demand. If you have no hard
disk in your computer, you can ignore the subdirectory commands until you
get one. If someone else takes care of backing up data and program files, you
won't need to know about **BACKUP**, **RESTORE**, or **XCOPY**. The commands that are generally most useful are described early in this book. The index, table of contents, and command index will help you locate additional information as needed.

How This Book is Organized

Figuring out what should be learned first is a central problem in developing a
familiarity with DOS. Here, the most commonly needed DOS commands and
concepts are isolated in the "Essential DOS Concepts" and "Essential DOS
Commands" chapters. "The DOS Shell" describes the features of IBM's new
menu-oriented user interface. "Useful DOS Commands and Concepts" explains the usage of less frequently required DOS capabilities. Brief descriptions of both the more advanced and the only occasionally useful DOS facilities are presented in the "Additional DOS Commands and Concepts" chapter.

Because of their importance, batch files are covered in a separate chapter. "Supplementing DOS" describes utility programs, many of them in the
public domain or available as low-cost shareware, that complement—or in
some cases replace—basic DOS commands. "DOS Tips and Tricks" is a grab

bag of occasionally useful and generally non-obvious techniques for making computer operation more convenient. As libraries begin to use CD-ROM products, a number of special DOS-related problems come to the fore. They are dealt with in the "CD-ROM and DOS" section.

Since DOS commands are discussed in order of usefulness rather than in alphabetical order, some means of quickly locating information about a particular command is needed. The Command Index provides a quick listing of DOS commands.

A glossary of terms is provided to help the new DOS user keep track of the terminology and concepts used elsewhere in the book.

Conventions

A number of typographic conventions are used in explanations of the syntax of DOS commands. Square brackets ([ ]) indicate optional text or numeric characters that the user may enter. The arrow brackets (< >) denote mandatory, user-entered characters. Commands—always presented in uppercase—will operate equally well in lowercase except as noted. Possible alternate values are separated by a vertical bar character (|).

In some contexts, the term "filespec" is used. Filespec is short for "file specification," which may contain any or all of the following: drive letter, path, filename, and filename extension.

In those few examples where its placement is important to understanding the action of a DOS command, the underline character is used to represent the cursor. The DOS prompt C>, or perhaps C:\BOOK>, is only shown when it will contribute to an understanding of topic under discussion. Readers should be aware that their DOS prompt will always display in the course of entering the command lines shown here.

A number of new commands and command options have been introduced in relatively recent versions of DOS. In many cases, a version number indicates which version first had the feature being described. It is assumed, and is generally true, that later versions of DOS support the features of their predecessors.

1

ESSENTIAL DOS CONCEPTS

Before we can discuss DOS commands in detail, we must be sure we are proceeding from a common understanding of some basic concepts concerning IBM-compatible personal computers in general and disk operating systems in particular.

Programs

A program is a set of instructions that tells a computer what to do. The instructions are recorded in a format that makes them "understandable" to, and executable by, DOS. Once the computer has been booted, a program is run by typing its filename. "Software" is a synonym for a program, or more often, a collection of related programs that work together.

A large, complex piece of software is just a combination of thousands of short, simple commands that "instructs" the computer to wait for a character from the keyboard, display that character on the screen, change the screen background color to red, wait for the user to strike the Enter key before causing a beep to issue from the speaker, etc. It is the blazing speed of the microprocessor in the computer that turns enormous, tedious lists of instructions into near-instantaneous magic.

Programs can be written in a variety of computer languages, the advantages and disadvantages of which are of little concern to us here. Indeed, once the original series of instructions created by a programmer is converted to machine language (i.e., compiled), the language used to create the instructions is irrelevant. The important point is that without DOS to manage things, no programs, no matter how well put together, would run.

DOS itself consists of a collection of programs, some of which are always active when the computer is running and others which only run when they are needed. In order to differentiate DOS programs and recognize their fundamental role in computer operation, they are sometimes called "system software." The programs for which we buy computers—the word processors, electronic spreadsheets, and card printing programs—belong in the category of "applications software."

Disk Drives

Disk drives are the most commonly used devices for permanently storing computer programs and the data they manipulate. Because disk drives play such a big role, and because their operation is so complex, the software that controls the operation of the computer as a whole is referred to as the disk operating system, or DOS.

Disk information is recorded as a sequence of codes electronically laid out on concentric tracks on two or more disk surfaces. Each code can represent any one of 256 different characters, some corresponding to the letters and numbers we are familiar with, others representing graphics characters, control functions, and other non-readable entities. A byte—one of those 256 possible codes—is equivalent to a character. A 360-kilobyte (KB) disk drive holds 360,000 bytes (or characters) worth of information—roughly 180 double-spaced, typewritten pages. A 20-megabyte (MB) drive stores 20,000,000 bytes, or roughly 10,000 double-spaced, typewritten pages.

There are two kinds of disk drives that are generally mounted inside a personal computer: floppy disk drives and hard (or fixed) disk drives. Floppy disk drives allow for the magnetic storage of information on a flexible mylar disk that is easily inserted and removed from a drive. A hard disk drive stores much more information, but is not removable.

Installing an internal floppy or hard disk drive is relatively easy. Experienced users can usually add or exchange a drive in 15–20 minutes using nothing more than a screwdriver. Those with little experience or self-confidence in such things should at least be aware of the ease and speed with which a dealer can change the disk storage capacity of a system.

Floppy Disks

The older, 5 1/4" variety of floppy disks comes in a bendable, non-removable jacket and stores either 360KB or 1,200KB (1.2MB), depending on whether it is rated for "double-density" or "high density." Generally, older machines that imitate the IBM PC/AT come with 1.2-MB floppy disk drives; you may specify a 360KB drive instead. Clones of the IBM PC/XT usually come with a 360-KB drive.

Like everything else having to do with computers, smaller is more beautiful. The 5 1/4" floppy disk drive is giving way to the 3 1/2" drive. This smaller drive has several advantages, including:

- computers that use 3 1/2" disk devices can be smaller and will take up less desk space
- the portable computers that use them are more compact, lighter, and consume less power
- more can be stored on the smaller disks
- they are enclosed in a rigid plastic shell with a metal shutter retarding entry of dust
- they can be carried in a shirt pocket without fear of damage

Here, too, there are two formats. IBM compatibles using the 8088 or 8086 microprocessors (XT compatibles) usually come with the 720-KB floppy drive. Systems based on the 80286 (AT compatibles) or 80386 microprocessors more often are accompanied by a 1.44-MB, 3 1/2" drive.

External floppy disk drives are becoming popular as a means of transferring disk files from a 3 1/2" disk to a 5 1/4" disk, or vice versa. In some setups the external drive can be readily moved from computer to computer as needed.

Hard Disk Drives

A hard disk drive differs from a floppy drive in three main respects: removability, speed, and capacity. There is no removable medium analogous to the floppy disk. Information stored on the surfaces of the several platters inside the case of the hard drive stays there. Programs can be loaded from disk and data saved to a hard disk from two to six times faster than with a floppy disk drive.

Again, hard disks store *much* more information than floppy disks. The smallest commercially offered drive as of this writing has a 20-MB capacity. A substantial body of users is paying the relatively small incremental difference to acquire 40-MB capacity instead. Meanwhile, drives that hold 60MB, 80MB, and 100MB are coming down steadily in price.

Most hard drives these days are internal. They are built into the same case as the microprocessor, power supply, and associated circuitry. Most computers allow for the addition of external disk drives. DOS allows you to refer to them as "D:," "E:," or some similar designation. It is rare that a hard drive needs to be attached externally due to insufficient room inside the computer case.

The Default Drive

Unless you tell it differently, DOS assumes that disk-related commands will act upon files stored on a specific drive: the "default drive." DOS makes the assumption that, for example, **DIR** alone is a request for a directory listing of files on the current default drive. To get a directory of files on drive B:, you must explicitly specify that drive: **DIR B:**. If you put a disk with the DOS files on it in drive A: and start up the computer, drive A: will be the default drive. This is indicated by the DOS prompt "A>." (Using the **PROMPT** command, discussed elsewhere in this book, the prompt can be changed to almost anything.)

If you boot from a hard disk drive—drive C: on virtually every IBM-compatible computer system—then C: will be the default drive. All commands will assume that files on drive C: are to be acted upon, unless the contrary is explicitly indicated by another drive designation. You can change the default drive simply by typing the designation of another drive. The system prompt will confirm the change:

```
A>  C:
C>
```

This process is sometimes referred to as "logging onto" a new drive.

Systems containing just one floppy disk drive must designate it as drive A:. That same drive can also behave like drive B:, however. You can log onto B: or use it for most other DOS operations. Thus, it is possible with a single-floppy system to enter **XCOPY A:*.* B:**. DOS will ask you to insert a disk for drive B: and strike any key to continue. In this way, you can do disk-to-disk copying, albeit with some disk swapping.

Booting the System

When you flip the power switch on the computer a small program contained on a read-only memory (ROM) chip on the computer's main circuit board attempts to locate and load the disk files containing the essential operating system components. When the program finds them, it places them in random-access memory (RAM) and passes control of the rest of the start-up process to them.

If the floppy disk door is closed, the computer attempts to load the operating system from the floppy disk in drive A:. If the floppy drive is open and a hard disk is present, system files are loaded from the hard disk.

Should the computer get stuck due to a software problem or hardware glitch, it may be necessary to restart from the beginning. This is called "rebooting" the computer. You could turn the power switch off, wait a few seconds (always a good idea), then turn it on again. This, however, is cumbersome and time-consuming. It is faster and causes less wear and tear on the hard disk to perform a "warm boot" by holding down the Ctrl and Alt keys and pressing the Del key. The system goes back almost—but not quite—to the beginning of the boot process followed when the machine was first turned on.

It is often necessary to reboot the system after making modifications required in conjunction with installation of new software. Only after rebooting do any new configuration settings take effect. Many IBM PC-compatible computers (but—as of this writing—not IBM PCs) offer still another means of rebooting the computer without turning it off. They feature a "reset" button, frequently located on the front panel of the system. The reset button will restart the system when, because of the nature of the hang up, the Ctrl-Alt-Del combination fails to do so.

Files

The bytes and kilobytes of information stored on disk drives are organized into discrete units called "files." A file may consist of the program, i.e., the instructions, that causes word-processing software to behave like word-processing software. It may consist of the alphabetic characters that make up the contents of a letter created with the word-processing program. All data that you may store on a disk is stored as a file. Files may be as small as one byte or as large as your disk drive's capacity will allow. DOS commands manipulate information largely by acting upon files.

File Naming

Each file has to have a name. DOS is stingy, though. It allows only eight characters for a filename, plus three characters for an optional filename extension. Where it is present, the filename extension is separated from the rest of the filename by a period.

When you are asked to specify a filename, it is imperative that you use a name that is meaningful to you. LETTER11 may make perfect sense today, but three months from now when you want to locate the file again, SMITH-JOB.LTR will be much more helpful.

While you may specify whatever file extension you like for many files, there are some important exceptions. The following extensions are reserved. They have special meaning and should not be used for purposes other than those listed:

.COM   Computer program; immediately executable

.EXE   Computer program; immediately executable

.BAT   Batch file containing DOS commands or programs (or both); immediately executable (see chapter on batch files for more information)

.SYS   System device drivers or other special files used to configure the computer system at the time it is booted

You should be aware of popular conventions for assignment of filename extensions that have developed over the years. DOS won't complain if you deviate from "standard practice," but you risk considerable confusion:

.OVR   An overlay file; a part of a large program stored as a separate file and only loaded when required; used to conserve random-access memory space

.BAK   A backup version of a file; some word-processing programs automatically create .BAK files every time a text file is saved; when it comes time to prune those files by deleting everything with a .BAK extension, everything will go, whatever the source of the extension

.BK!   Like .BAK, above

.DBF   dBase data file

.PRG   dBase program file

.FRM   dBase format file

.WKS   Lotus worksheet file

.CAL   SuperCalc worksheet file

Be sensitive to conventions in filenaming. Avoid the patterns used by the designers of DOS and of your applications programs. Develop a system of your own that will tell you the contents of files just from the name.

Internal vs. External Commands

DOS commands are either internal or external. Internal commands are built into that portion of the operating system that is always running when you are at the DOS prompt. When you type commands—for example, **COPY** or **DIR**—DOS finds and activates the appropriate program routines. Since these relatively simple program segments are already sitting in RAM, they can be executed very quickly.

External commands, on the other hand, are not instantly on tap. They are stored in separate files as discrete programs that must be explicitly loaded and run like any other applications program. To run **XCOPY**, an enhanced copy utility supplied with newer versions of DOS, you type its name. If **XCOPY.EXE** is in either the current directory or a directory named in a PATH list, it will be run. If it is not available on disk, "Bad Command or Filename" will be DOS' reply.

The more complicated and less frequently used DOS commands tend to be external. The simpler and more frequently required commands are mostly internal.

Wildcards

Wildcards are special symbols that replace one or more characters in a file-name specification and allow the user to specify multiple files to those DOS commands that can work with more than one file at a time. If you need infor-mation about a file but don't know the full name, wildcards can help you get information as well.

The asterisk (*) replaces any number of characters to the right of as many characters of the filename or filename extension as you care to type. To produce a directory listing of files with a .BAK extension, enter **DIR C:*.BAK**. To delete all files beginning with OLD, type **DEL A:OLD*.***. The question mark (?) replaces any single character in the file-name or filename extension. To copy files LETR1JUN, LETR4JUN, and LETR5JUN to A:, you would type **COPY C:LETR?JUN A:**. Both wild-cards can be used together. To delete LETR files with either a .BAK or .BK file extension, you could enter **DEL C:LETR?JUN.B***.

Further examples of wildcard uses are included in the discussion of indi-vidual commands that make use of them. You must be particularly careful in

employing wildcards in file deletion. It is too easy to forget that some category of file that you do not wish to delete matches the specification given.
When in doubt, check before you delete:

DIR C:LETR?.B*
DEL C:LETR?.B*

Formatting

Before a hard disk or a floppy disk can be used to store computer data, it must
be formatted. Formatting lays out a framework of tracks and sectors across the
surface(s) of the disk, and the file allocation table and directory structure used
in locating specific material stored in those sectors and tracks. Formatting is a
lot like painting lines on a newly paved parking lot to guide the drivers that
will be using it. Only when this framework is complete can DOS store files
on a disk.

Floppy disks are formatted using the **FORMAT** command, the partic-
ulars of which are discussed elsewhere. **FORMAT** command is also used in
conjunction with hard disks. Use of this command is the third step in prepar-
ing a hard disk for use. The first is low-level formatting. The hard drive manufacturer or supplier will provide you with directions for invoking a low-level
format routine. Often, the routine is stored in read-only memory on the hard
disk controller card and must be run using the DOS DEBUG program.

The second step is the partitioning of the disk. The DOS **FDISK** command allows you to divide a single hard disk drive into more than one logical
drive, creating drives C: and D: on a single physical device. If your hard drive
can store more than 32MB of data, and you use DOS 3.3 or lower, you will
have to partition your drive into two or more logical drives in order to use its
full capacity. DOS 4.0 allows for larger partitions.

Those using UNIX or some other operating system in addition to DOS
will also want to partition their hard drive into one drive for each environment.

Most computer dealers will perform all three steps prior to delivery of a
purchased system. If you are buying a system with a hard drive with greater
than 32-MB capacity, and will be using it with a version of DOS lower than
4.0, you should be aware that you may specify the size of each logical drive.
Two 20-MB drives may be preferable for some applications, while a 32-MB

and an 8-MB may be better for others. Maybe three drives—C:, D:, and E:— would be the ideal situation. Unless you tell the dealer what to do, you will get his or her best guess as to what will satisfy your needs.

Configuring the System

The CONFIG.SYS file is the key to setting up DOS the way your programs require it. Whenever the computer is booted, DOS looks for a CONFIG.SYS file. If it finds the file, it executes the configuring instructions contained therein before proceeding any further.

Many programs require a minimum number of memory "buffers," segments of random-access memory used to hold data on its way to or from the disk drives. Others must be able to have more disk files open than DOS would normally allow. The following lines in the CONFIG.SYS file set these parameters to commonly used values:

BUFFERS=20
FILES=15

DOS allows you to use CONFIG.SYS to install one or more device drivers—software modules that give DOS the ability to work with hardware and software it does not otherwise support. The capability to work with a CD-ROM drive is often added with a line such as:

DEVICE=\DEV\HITACHI.SYS /D:MSCD000 /N:1

Additional screen manipulation capabilities become available to programs if the ANSI.SYS screen-writing device driver provided with DOS is installed as the system is booted. The VDISK.SYS device driver, also included with DOS, sets up an electronic imitation of a disk drive in part of the system's random-access memory.

Tape drives, Write Once/Read Many (WORM) optical drives, and local-area networks are among the other devices that may be supported with manufacturer-provided device drivers possibly included in CONFIG.SYS.

For a detailed description of the commands that go into a CONFIG.SYS file, see "Configuring the System" in the chapter on Useful DOS Commands and Concepts.

Automating the System

After looking for CONFIG.SYS, DOS seeks a file called AUTOEXEC.BAT. If it finds the file, it executes the commands found there before doing anything else. You can run applications programs and execute DOS commands one after the other from within the AUTOEXEC.BAT file. It is possible to set up AUTOEXEC.BAT so that a word-processing program is automatically loaded and run as soon as the computer is turned on. The user need not even know the program's filename.

The AUTOEXEC.BAT file is an extremely important tool in making a computer system easier and more convenient to use. Consult the "Batch Files" chapter for information on how to create and modify AUTOEXEC.BAT. The discussion of individual DOS commands will indicate those that are often included in an AUTOEXEC.BAT.

The Keyboard

There are numerous keyboard layouts used with IBM PC-compatible computers. Some keyboards have a separate numeric keypad, while others employ the same keys both to represent numbers and to control cursor movement. Some have 10 function keys at the left of the keyboard, while others have 10 or 12 function keys across the top.

All keyboards have a PrtSc key. Shift-PrtSc sends an image of the current screen display to the printer. Ctrl-PrtSc turns on the printer echo feature whereby every character appearing on the screen is also printed. Pressing Ctrl-PrtSc a second time turns the printer echo off. Ctrl-P has the same effect as Ctrl-PrtSc. Every keyboard has a Break key. Batch files, many DOS commands, and some applications programs can be halted or exited (or both) by pressing Ctrl-Break while they are running. In some circumstances Ctrl-C has the same effect.

There is an escape key (Esc) on every IBM PC-compatible keyboard. Its only function at the DOS level is to abandon a previously typed DOS command line and start a new one. Typing some gibberish followed by the escape key yields:

```
C:\>  ;jfkjhkdjfshkj\
      _
```

When you **TYPE** the contents of a long text file, or produce a long file list with **DIR**, text scrolls off the display screen faster than you can read it. To pause the scrolling, type Ctrl-S. Pressing any other key will restart scrolling. Most IBM PC-compatible keyboards have Scroll Lock keys that don't work.

The function keys have primitive use in editing the DOS command line. The only one I've found to be of any value at all is F3. Pressing F3 at the DOS prompt causes the most recently typed DOS command to reappear. Most users will ignore the function keys and retype an incorrect command line instead.

The Microprocessor

The microprocessor—the "brains" of a personal computer—is a single computer chip containing the circuitry necessary to control the functioning of the rest of the computer. It executes the instructions contained in DOS and applications programs. While they are being executed, program instructions are stored temporarily in random-access memory.

IBM's personal computers make use of the Intel series of microprocessors. The IBM PC and PC/XT used the 8088 microprocessor chip; the IBM PC/AT used the 80286. The PS/2 Models 25 and 30 use a close relative, the 8086 chip; models 50 and 60 use the 80286; and models 70 and 80 contain the powerful 80386. By the time you read this, IBM undoubtedly will have added new models and discontinued some older ones. The trend is toward making the 80286 the low-end standard. The Intel 80486 will eventually find its way into the line at the high—i.e., expensive—end.

Microprocessors are distinguished by the amount of information they are able to work with at one time and by the clock-rate at which they operate. The 8086 and 80286 work with 16 bits of data (two bytes) at a time. Internally, the 8088 also works with two bytes, but it can only transfer data one byte (eight bits) at a time to other chips in the system. The 80386 can work with 32 bits (four bytes) at a time, considerably increasing the amount of data processing the system can accomplish.

The speed at which the microprocessor operates is continually being increased. Makers of IBM compatibles compete in large part by attempting to out-perform the original article on the basis of speed. Whatever speed ratings I set down here will be superceded by the time you read this. Suffice it to say that you must balance the desirability of increased speed against the increased cost of that speed.

Memory

Just about everything a computer does involves the microprocessor and memory. Programs are copied from disk into random-access memory (RAM) where the instructions they contain can be executed by the processor. Data stored on disk are copied into RAM, manipulated, then "saved" back to disk where they may safely reside until needed once again.

RAM consists physically of fingernail-sized computer chips enclosed in insect-like "dual in-line packages" (DIPs). Rows of skinny metallic contacts project downward along the two long edges of the rectangular packages. The contacts fit into matching sockets located either on the computer's main circuit board (the "motherboard") or on an expansion card plugged into one of the slots provided for that purpose on the motherboard. As systems use more and more memory, new packaging approaches are beginning to appear. Sockets and single chips are still the rule, however.

Memory chips must match the speed of the microprocessor in use. The faster the microprocessor, the more expensive the memory chips.

Compatibility

DOS is not a program associated solely, or even primarily, with computers manufactured by IBM. When it introduced it's Personal Computer, complete with DOS 1.0, IBM invented a category. In the years since, hundreds of companies have rushed in to imitate, and in some cases improve upon, the original article.

The development and marketing of personal computers highly similar to the IBM PCs ("IBM compatibles") has been successful for computer makers because of the thousands of useful and powerful software packages created for that system. Discerning purchasers have been attracted by the lower prices and more state-of-the-art features that some compatibles designers have incorporated in their offerings. As of this writing, estimates put IBM's share of the IBM compatibles market at below 40 percent.

Compatibility is a slippery thing. At one time, you could test compatibility by determining whether a given software package or hardware device worked on a compatible the same way it worked a comparable IBM system. With IBM's introduction of a new line of computers (Personal System/2)—the more powerful of which will not accept the same interface cards as the IBM PC/XT/AT—hardware compatibility is a matter of definition: either IBM is no longer IBM-compatible, or there are no more IBM compatibles other than those that mimic the Micro Channel Architecture.

Leaving aside the hardware issues for the moment, it is still possible to test software compatibility. A highly compatible computer ought to run IBM-marketed versions of DOS interchangeably with Microsoft versions available from third-party sources. Microsoft Flight Simulator, a highly popular game program, is commonly used to test the ability of a compatible to handle complex graphics.

Shells

Much of what follows concerns the various commands that DOS provides for manipulation of disk files. Mastery of the essentials comes fairly quickly. There is no denying, however, that the first few sessions in which you attempt to work at the operating system level—outside of the word processor or database manager you run most of the time—can result in confusion and frustration.

DOS sits there with its smug, minimal prompt waiting for you to tell it what to do. "I'm a beginner," you want to say. "Give me some suggestions. Give me a clue!" DOS is an essay exam in a situation where we would all appreciate a multiple-choice quiz instead. Wouldn't learning DOS be simpler if our alternatives were listed and we could pick from among them? Notwithstanding the comprehension of DOS concepts required to make full use of the menu options presented by a shell, everyday DOS functions would still be easier to learn within a menu-based framework.

Third-party developers have recognized the need for a DOS Shell for some time. Xtree and XtreePro from Executive Systems are two among many excellent shells that make working with disk files far easier than would otherwise be the case. Still River Shell, developed by Bill White, is a shareware ("try before you buy") shell that is widely available from bulletin boards and public-domain software libraries. IBM itself finally acknowledged the utility of such an approach when it provided the DOS Shell with version 4.0 of DOS. Now that the trend-setter in operating system design for IBM compatibles has endorsed the shell-based approach, you can expect to see it supercede the commands described here. Copying, renaming, viewing, deleting, and finding files can all be done quite easily within a well-designed shell. Less frequently required operations may not be as well provided for in the shell.

See the "DOS Shell" chapter for a description of the DOS 4.0 Shell, and the chapter on "Supplementing DOS" for more about shells in general.

2

ESSENTIAL DOS COMMANDS

Presented here are the most frequently required DOS commands. Whatever your special needs may be, it is extremely difficult to make effective use of a computer without a grasp of the function and syntax of the handful of commands discussed in the coming pages.

The essential DOS commands, without which a user of IBM PC compatibles would be severely hampered, are:

DIR	for producing a directory listing of files
CHKDSK	for reporting statistics on disk usage and remedying a limited range of disk file problems
FORMAT	for preparing new disks for use
COPY	(or the enhanced version called **XCOPY**) for moving files either between disk drives or—less commonly—between a computer "device" and a disk file
DEL/ERASE	for deleting unneeded disk files
REN/RENAME	for changing the name of an existing disk file
TYPE	for displaying the contents of a text file on the screen
DATE and **TIME**	for setting the system date and time used by the computer when it "stamps" a new file
DOSSHELL	the batch file that invokes the new DOS Shell in DOS 4.0
SELECT	a command new with DOS 4.0 that automates the process of installing a new version of DOS and setting various defaults that are to be used with it

> **DIR**
> **Directory**

SYNTAX: DIR [drive:] [file specification] [/P | /W]

PURPOSE: Displays a list of the disk files meeting the file specification. If no file specification is entered, the contents of the current drive and subdirectory are shown. (Internal)

SWITCHES: /P Pause directory display when screen fills, restart when any key is struck.

/W Display the list of files in five columns across the width of the screen, showing filenames but no dates or file sizes.

USAGE: To display a list of all the files on the current default drive and directory, type: **C:\> DIR.**

```
Volume in drive C has no label
Directory of C:

.                  <DIR>          1-20-88     8:30p
..                 <DIR>          1-20-88     8:30p
INDEX     DOS        256          9-10-88    11:01a
ADDL      BAK       2176          9-18-88    12:04a
GLOSS     BAK      18688          9-17-88    10:08p
JUNK      BAT        110          9-18-88     4:49p
TEST      SRT        756          9-20-88     9:44p
TREE      FI        4096          9-18-88     5:43p
JUNK4               2052          9-18-88     3:35p
TREELIST           56647          9-18-88     5:45p
BATCH     BAK      14976          9-21-88     9:02p
TEST      FIL        768          9-20-88     9:43p
TEST      REV        756          9-20-88     9:46p
SORT                 216          9-20-88     9:50p
BATCH     DOS      14976          9-21-88     9:14p
USEFUL    DOS      55552          9-20-88    10:43p
ESSEN     BAK      45184          9-24-88     9:06a
          15 File(s)   3512320 bytes free
```

"Volume in drive C has no label" refers to the absence of an optional internal label. Labels are designed to identify disks internally, thereby making it simple to identify a disk even if its external, stick-on label has been lost. Since adhesive labels generally don't fall off, few users employ electronic labels. The only obvious use for such labels is in the automated cataloging of a large library of disks. See the discussion of **VOL** and **LABEL** (under "Miscellaneous") in the "Useful DOS Commands and Concepts" chapter and the description of the /V parameter used with **FORMAT** (in this chapter).

In the above display, the first two columns contain the filename and filename extension of each file on drive C:. Notice that directory listings separate the filename and its extension by spaces. In all other contexts, filename and filename extension must be separated by a period and no spaces.

The third column shows the file size in bytes. The date and time that the file was last changed occupy the last two columns. DOS automatically applies a time/date stamp to every file it writes to disk, based on the current setting of its built-in clock/calendar function. If your computer has no battery-backed internal clock, you will have to set the date and time every time you turn on or reboot the computer (**DATE** and **TIME** commands are discussed later).

To display a list of files on drive A:, type **DIR A:**. Wildcards can be used with **DIR**. To show all files on drive C: with an extension of .BAK, type: **DIR C:*.BAK**.

Volume in drive C has no label
Directory of C:

```
ADDL     BAK      2176    9-18-88   12:04a
GLOSS    BAK     18688    9-17-88   10:08p
BATCH    BAK     14976    9-21-88    9:02p
ESSEN    BAK     45184    9-24-88    9:06a
        4 File(s) 3506176 bytes free
```

To list files on the same drive with an extension of BKK, BCK, or BAK, type: **DIR C:*.B?K**.

Volume in drive C has no label
Directory of C:

```
ADDL     BAK      2176    9-18-88   12:04a
GLOSS    BAK     18688    9-17-88   10:08p
JUNK     BCK       110    9-18-88    4:49p
BATCH    BAK     14976    9-21-88    9:02p
ESSEN    BAK     45184    9-24-88    9:06a
        5 File(s) 3502080 bytes free
```

Hidden files and system files are not listed by **DIR**. If you wish a hidden file to be shown by **DIR**, use the **ATTRIB** command to change its status.

It is sometimes helpful to create a text file containing a list of the information reported by **DIR**. This is easily done using the output redirection operator, ">." To send the result of a directory listing request to a disk file

called DIRECTRY.LST, type: **DIR C:*.BAK > DIRECTRY.LST**.
If you wish to add to an existing DIRECTRY.LST file, then the ">>" operator will come in handy: **DIR C:*.BAK >> BIGFILE.LST**.

The ability to build a list of filenames can be very useful to any user who
has reason to create batch files that perform extensive delete and copy operations.

CHKDSK
Checks Disk

SYNTAX: CHKDSK [drive:][filespec] [/F I /V]

PURPOSE: (1) Displays disk capacity, number of bytes in hidden files
(usually the operating system files), number of bytes in subdirectory entries,
number of subdirectories, number of bytes in "user" (i.e. ordinary) files, number of files, number of bytes available on disk; (2) displays total system random-access memory and amount currently available for use by programs; (3)
tests for errors in file allocation table (the FAT) and the disk's directory; (4)
remedies some errors relating to the FAT and directory; and (5) lists requested
files with complete pathname. (External)

SWITCHES: / F Fixes any errors it finds. Without the /F parameter,
 CHKDSK only *seems* to fix errors.
 / V Displays list of all files, with complete pathname. Can
 be used in conjunction with redirection operator ">" to
 create a text file with the names of files on a disk.

USAGE: Entering **CHKDSK C:**, under DOS 3.2, produces the following
display:

```
33419264    bytes    total disk space
   47104    bytes    in 2 hidden files
  133120    bytes    in 59 directories
28131328    bytes    in 1253 user files
  112640    bytes    in bad sectors
 4995072    bytes    available on disk

  655360    bytes    total memory
  506448    bytes    free
```

Note that "bad sectors"—not infrequently present on hard disk drives—

are not a cause for alarm unless they constitute a significant portion of disk capacity, or suddenly and unaccountably begin increasing in number.

FORMAT
Prepares Disk for Use

SYNTAX: FORMAT [drive:] [/S | /F:<size> | /V | /V:<label> | /B | /4 | / 1 | /8 | /N | /T]

PURPOSE: Prepares a new disk or a hard disk drive for receipt of data. (External)

SWITCHES: **/ S** Create bootable disk by copying system files and COM-MAND.COM to disk after formatting.

/F:<size> Specifies capacity to which disk is to be format ted if less than maximum drive capacity.

/ V Prompt the user for an optional 11-character volume label to be attached to the formatted disk.

/V:<label> Specifies volume label rather than waiting for **FORMAT** to prompt for volume label (DOS 4.0).

/ B Reserve space for system files which will be added later using the **SYS** command.

/ 4 Format a 360-KB disk for use at that capacity in a 1.2-MB floppy drive.

/ 1 Format just one side of disk so it can be used in a single-sided floppy disk drive.

/ 8 Format at eight sectors per track rather than the usual nine, providing compatibility with older 320-KB disk formats.

/N:nn Number of sectors per track.

/T:nn Number of tracks on the disk.

USAGE: To format a disk in drive A:, type **FORMAT A:**. To create a bootable 720-KB disk using a 1.44-MB drive, type: **FORMAT A: /S / F:720**. The following command lines are identical; they direct the formatting of a 360-KB floppy using a 1.2-MB drive, and prompt the user for a volume label:

    FORMAT A: /4 /V
    FORMAT A: /F:360 /V

CAUTION: **FORMAT** wipes out information already recorded on a disk. It should be used carefully. *Be sure to specify the drive to be formatted.* If you don't, **FORMAT** will attempt to format the currently logged drive, perhaps obliterating the contents of your hard drive. Heed the request for confirmation that DOS always makes prior to executing **FORMAT**. The computer will follow the directions it has been given, not those the user has meant to give.

While there is utility software on the market that can sometimes rescue part of what has been lost (see the "Supplementing DOS" chapter), this is a far chancier situation than simply recovering an erased file. Assume that **FORMAT** is forever and act accordingly.

COPY
Copies a File

SYNTAX: COPY [[drive:][filespec]] [[drive:][filespec]] [/A I /B I /V I /P]

PURPOSE: (1) Copies disk files from one disk or subdirectory to another; (2) copies data from a disk file to the printer or other device; (3) concatenates (combines) several files into one; and (4) copies data from the console or other device to a file. (Internal)

SWITCHES: / A Treat as an ASCII text file, copying only up to the first end-of-file character.
/ B Treat as a binary file, copying the entire file irrespective of end-of-file markers.
/ V Verify that the copy operation was completed properly. Offers extra security, though **COPY** operations are generally pretty reliable.
/ P Prompt user for confirmation on copying of each file.

USAGE: To copy a single file from one drive to another, type: **COPY A:WS.EXE   B:WS.EXE.** You can change the filename in the copying process: **COPY A:WS.EXE   B:WSBACKUP.EXE.**

Wildcards can be used to copy multiple files in one step. If there is no filename change, the destination filename can be omitted: **COPY A:*.*** **C:.** You can omit the drive designation if the current default drive is the one intended. To copy all the files that end in .BAK from B: to A:, where A: is the default drive, type:

```
A>
A> COPY B:*.BAK
```

A simple way to selectively back up files is to use wildcards in combination with the /P switch. The following command cycles through all the files on the current drive and directory, allowing the user to decide individually which files will actually be copied and which will be skipped: **COPY A:*.* B: /P.**

You can print a text file—one containing no control characters—using the **COPY** command. Only legitimate DOS printer device names can be used: PRN, LPT1, and LPT2: **COPY A:MYLIST.TXT PRN.**

To combine several text files into one, type:

COPY A:TEXT1+A:TEXT2+A:TEXT3   B:TEXT.ALL

To append the contents of TEXT2 and TEXT3 to TEXT1, you could type:

COPY A:TEXT1+A:TEXT2+A:TEXT3

A small text file can be quickly and conveniently created using the **COPY** command. Let's say you want to create a new AUTOEXEC.BAT batch file that will automatically run WordStar when the computer is turned on. The folowing text, followed by Ctrl-Z (or F6, which sends a Ctrl-Z end-of-file marker), will create an appropriate AUTOEXEC.BAT:

```
COPY CON AUTOEXEC.BAT
PATH  C:\UTIL;C:\BIN;C:\DOS;C:\;c:\WS5;c:\DBASE
PROMPT $p$_$g
TIMER/S
\BIN\MSCDEX.EXE /D:MSCD000  /M:8   ^Z
```

You can work on only one line at a time using **COPY CON**. Once the Enter key has been struck, there is no way to get back to the line above and change something. There is no way to edit an existing text file with **COPY CON** either. A new **COPY CON** AUTOEXEC.BAT wipes out the entire contents of the previously existing AUTOEXEC.BAT. Most people find a word processor or editor preferable to **COPY CON** for all but the shortest batch files. You may even wish to investigate **EDLIN**—a minimalist line editor included free with DOS—that at least allows you to edit rather than retype text files when changes are necessary.

Note: If you copy to a destination filename that is already in use, the old file is overwritten by the source file. *Beware:* DOS gives you no warning, no chance to reconsider. If you are attempting to back up the latest version of THESIS.TXT to a floppy in drive A:, you could ruin your day by reversing the order of source and destination filespecs and typing the following:

COPY A:THESIS.TXT   C:THESIS.TXT

You may find it safer to change filenames when backing up a file:

COPY C:THESIS.TXT   A:THESISBK.TXT

XCOPY
Enhanced Copy Utility

SYNTAX: XCOPY [drive:][filespec] [drive:][filespec] [/A ǀ /D:date ǀ /E ǀ /M ǀ /P ǀ /S ǀ /V ǀ /W]

PURPOSE: Copies files in ways not possible with the **COPY** command. (External)

SWITCHES: / A Copy files with archive bit set on, but don't change the archive bit subsequent to copying.
/ D Copy only those files with a date the same as or later than the designated date.
/ E Copy subdirectories even if they are empty.
/ M Copy files with archive bit set on, then turn the archive bit off.
/ P Prompt for user approval for copying of each file.
/ S Copy all designated files in the specified directory and all files in subdirectories of that directory. Empty subdirectories are not copied.
/ V Verify that copy operation was successful.
/ W Wait for user to insert disk before beginning copying.

USAGE: XCOPY comes into its own on systems with a hard disk drive. For an introduction to subdirectories, see the section on hard disk use in the "Useful DOS Commands and Concepts" chapter. **XCOPY** is quicker and more powerful than **COPY**. While the variety of options available with it can be confusing at first, learning to use them will be well worth the effort. **XCOPY** can be used in place of **BACKUP** to produce backup copies of important data and program files. While **BACKUP** saves files in a format that can only be used with **RESTORE**, **XCOPY** leaves the files in their normal DOS format.

XCOPY won't handle files that are larger than the capacity of a floppy disk and it won't automatically format a floppy disk. If you run out of disk space on the target disk, **XCOPY** will report "insufficient disk space" and stop dead in its tracks. It would be far more helpful if it would prompt for a second disk.

To copy files from several subdirectories while preserving the subdirectory structure, use the /S switch. If you would like even empty subdirectories to be copied, add the /E switch:

XCOPY C:\DBXL A:\   /S   /E

All the usual wildcards will work with **XCOPY**. Here we copy all the files ending in .DOS that have their archive bit set on:

XCOPY C:\BOOK*.DOS   A: /A

If we had wanted to turn the archive bit off as part of the copying process, we would have used /M in place of /A. If you use the prompt switch (/ P) you can cycle through all your files, with **XCOPY** asking you one at a time which one to copy. To copy only those files created after a specified date, type:

XCOPY   C:\BOOK A: /D:09-23-88

XCOPY is faster than **COPY** at copying multiple files.

> **DEL/ERASE**
> **Deletes a File**

SYNTAX: DEL [drive:] <filespec> [/P]

PURPOSE: Deletes disk files that are no longer needed. (Internal)

SWITCHES: / P Prompts the user for approval of deletion of each specified file. (DOS 4.0)

USAGE: To delete a single file, type: **DEL LETTER.BAK**. To erase all files on a disk or within a given subdirectory:

> **DEL B:*.***
> **Are you sure? (Y/N)**
> **Y**

Utility software is available that will unerase deleted files if new data has not been subsequently recorded over them.

```
REN/RENAME
Renames a File
```

SYNTAX: REN [drive:] [filespec] [filename]

PURPOSE: Renames one or more files. (Internal)

USAGE: To change NEWLIST to OLDLIST, type **RENAME A:NEWLIST OLDLIST**. Wildcards can be used to rename multiple files: **REN *.LTR *.BAK**.

```
TYPE
Displays File Contents
```

SYNTAX: TYPE [drive:] <filespec>

PURPOSE: Displays the contents of a text file on the display screen. Use Ctrl-S to pause the scrolling display. (Internal)

USAGE: To view the contents of a documentation file, presumably an AS-CII text file, type: **TYPE README.DOC**.

TYPE can be made to pause automatically every time the screen fills up. The following command line "pipes" the lines from README.DOC to the **MORE** command:

TYPE README.DOC | MORE

For a full discussion of **MORE** and other ways of redirecting the output of one command to some other destination, see the section on filters and piping in the "Useful DOS Commands and Concepts" chapter.

LIST is an excellent shareware replacement for **TYPE**. It offers numerous advantages and is well worth the small registration cost for those frequently using the **TYPE** command. For more information, see the "Supplementing DOS" chapter.

> **DATE**
> Sets   Date

SYNTAX: DATE [month-day-year]

PURPOSE: Displays the current system date and offers the user the opportunity to change the date. (Internal)

USAGE: Dates are entered with leading zeros if necessary, e.g. 09-01-89, not 9-1-89. The **DATE** command can be included in the AUTOEXEC.BAT file to automatically prompt the user for date whenever the computer is booted. Newer computers with a built-in, real-time clock-calendar generally come with a short program that will set the system clock from the internal real-time clock. The program, called RDCLOCK, GETCLOCK, or a similar name, is invoked from the AUTOEXEC.BAT file whenever the computer is booted.

> **TIME**
> Sets   Time

SYNTAX: TIME [hour:minutes:seconds:hundredths of a second]

PURPOSE: Displays the current system time and offers the user the opportunity to change the time. (Internal)

USAGE: Where necessary, leading zeros are used in specifying time. The **TIME** command can be included in the AUTOEXEC.BAT file to automatically prompt the user for time whenever the computer is booted. Newer computers with a built-in, real-time clock-calendar generally come with a short program that will set the system clock from the internal real-time clock. A program called RDCLOCK, GETCLOCK, or a similar name, is invoked from the AUTOEXEC.BAT file.

```
┌─────────────────────┐
│        CLS          │
│   Clears  Screen    │
└─────────────────────┘
```

SYNTAX: CLS

PURPOSE: Clears the display screen and shows the DOS prompt in the upper left-hand corner. (Internal)

USAGE: Users of older versions of DOS often use **CLS** in batch files to suppress the display of output from certain commands; the **ECHO OFF** command, designed to turn off screen output, appears onscreen. If you don't have a version of DOS that allows you to solve the problem by typing **@ECHO OFF**, then you have to type **ECHO OFF** followed by **CLS** to maintain a neat, blank screen. Maybe **CLS** isn't really as "essential" as some of the other commands in this section. It is simple and can reduce the visual clutter on-screen, thereby aiding the user in seeing more clearly what is going on.

```
┌─────────────────────┐
│     DOSSHELL        │
│  Invokes  DOS Shell │
└─────────────────────┘
```

SYNTAX: DOSSHELL

PURPOSE: Loads and runs the DOS Shell, a menu-based user interface designed to make learning and using DOS easier. (External, DOS 4.0)

USAGE: The DOS Shell, only available with DOS 4.0 and subsequent versions, allows for selection of DOS functions from a system of menus. It also allows the user to construct menus to automate the running of other programs stored in the system. See the "DOS Shell" chapter for a discussion of the operation of this important new addition to the standard DOS package.

   DOSSHELL is actually the filename of a batch file that makes use of several other programs provided as part of the DOS package. The DOS Shell may be activated by a batch file with another name of the user's choice.

```
┌──────────────────────────┐
│        SELECT            │
│  Installs/Configures  DOS │
└──────────────────────────┘
```

SYNTAX: SELECT

PURPOSE: Installs new version of DOS and customizes DOS to user's needs. (External, DOS 4.0)

USAGE: Put the DOS installation disk in drive A: and turn on or reset the computer. **SELECT** is automatically called from the AUTOEXEC.BAT file provided by IBM. The user answers the series of questions posed by **SE-LECT** regarding system configuration. **SELECT** can be run subsequently to modify DOS settings.

3

THE DOS SHELL

DOS 4.0 contains a number of major enhancements over previous versions of DOS. By far the most important for new users, however, is the "DOS Shell," a menu-based control system placed between the user and the various file manipulation commands discussed elsewhere in this book.

DOS has been derided for the difficulty many users encounter in learning the meaning and syntax of its diverse commands. Until now, the only way you could activate a command or run an applications program was by typing it's name, and its necessary parameters, in proper format. If you don't know what the proper format is, it's back to the manual. Only the fact that most users spend their time within one or two application programs—and can limp along without spending a great deal of time at the DOS level—has held the outcry against DOS' user-peculiar ways within bounds.

The key to making DOS commands easier to learn lies in making their existence and options obvious through a menu-oriented approach. With menus, it is often possible to determine which command is needed by process of elimination. Any student will tell you: multiple-choice tests are easier than short-answer tests. As a bonus, a menu structure also makes a good system of online help feasible.

IBM has finally seen the light, introducing a DOS Shell as part of version 4.0 of DOS. While far from ground-breaking (XtreePro from Executive Systems and Norton Commander from Peter Norton Computing are among the more popular of dozens of third-party shells that have been on the market for several years), IBM's efforts are especially significant as users now have the closest thing to an agreed-upon standard for such a menu-based interface. Some shell programs, including IBM's, also include menu-making capabilities. Once you've gained a bit of experience, you will be able to add to, delete from, and rearrange the menus within the DOS Shell that indicate what actions you may wish to take. A well thought-out system of menus can make use of your personal computer far more convenient than otherwise possible.

With a DOS Shell, there is always the risk that users will be able to avoid learning some basic command or concept that would simplify or improve their work. This line of argument asserts that ignorance is only bliss until you do something dumb that could have been avoided through learning DOS the "old-fashioned" way. The more puritanical among us will be cheered, however, as they realize that a significant level of DOS knowledge is necessary to make the fullest possible use of the menu-making capabilities of the 4.0 Shell.

In my view, the DOS Shell gives users a means of making greater use of DOS facilities earlier in their involvement with the computer. There will be enough instances in which a task can be done more quickly and easily from the DOS prompt that users will naturally begin to "exit to DOS" to make use of the myriad individual DOS commands discussed in this book. While the DOS Shell makes learning easier, it can also slow down an experienced user. The DOS Shell doesn't change the fact that for experienced users, "ease of use" often translates to the availability of efficient, command-driven shortcuts.

Starting the Shell

If you install DOS 4.0 with the **SELECT** utility, a batch file named DOS-SHELL.BAT will be created based on default settings determined by IBM's programmers and the answers to several of the questions asked as part of the user's interaction with **SELECT**.

To set the Shell running, simply type **DOSSHELL** at the system prompt. If you have reached a particular limitation of the Shell, you cannot use SELECT satisfactorily with your equipment, you want more control of the operation of the DOS Shell, or you're just curious, you will want to know how to customize the DOSSHELL.BAT to meet your needs.

As created through **SELECT**, DOSSHELL.BAT on my computer looks like this:

```
@SHELLB DOSSHELL
@IF ERRORLEVEL 255 GOTO END
:COMMON
@SHELLC  /MOS:PCIBMDRV.MOS/TRAN/COLOR
   /DOS/MENU/MUL/SND/MEU:SHELL.MEU/CLR:
   SHELL.CLR/PROMPT/MAINT/EXIT/SWAP/DATE
:END
@BREAK=ON
```

The programs SHELLB.EXE and SHELLC.EXE must be available

when DOSSHELL.BAT is run. The name of the batch file being executed—DOSSHELL.BAT in this case—must be specified with SHELLB in order for the Shell to operate properly. You can create multiple batch files with which to load the DOS Shell, each with its own customized settings. Just be sure the SHELLB line contains the name of the batch file in which it is present, in every case.

The key to setting up the Shell the way you want is the @SHELLC line. The parameters that it contains determine what the Shell will look like and how it will behave.

/MOS:PCIBMDRV.MOS specifies that the program necessary to drive the IBM mouse will be loaded. Drivers for several other popular mouse configurations are included. Only after the appropriate mouse driver is loaded is it possible to use the mouse to make menu selections.

/TRAN instructs the Shell to be transient rather than resident in memory. When you bring up the DOS prompt from within the Shell, memory that had been used by the Shell will be freed up for use by other programs. When you go back to the Shell, it will reload from disk. If the Shell is resident, menus jump into view faster after running a program. The Shell itself, however, takes considerable memory that would otherwise be available to applications programs. Some memory-hungry programs will only run if the Shell is transient.

/COLOR activates the Change Colors option on the Main Group menu.

/DOS activates File System on the Main Group menu.

/MENU activates Start Programs mode.

/MUL sets up for multiple file directory listings.

/SND enables sound.

/MEU specifies which menu file will be used by the Shell. Menu files can be created and edited from within the Shell or they can be supplied by a third-party source. The filename extension .MEU is automatically given to all menu files.

/CLR specifies filename of color setup to use.

/PROMPT enables option of exiting to DOS and returning.

/MAINT enables user to change program and group options.

/EXIT allows user to leave Shell completely using Exit option on action bar.

/SWAP directs the Shell to temporarily store information about files on disk while running a program or working from the DOS prompt. /SWAP speeds things up by avoiding the need to re-read the disk directory when coming back to the Shell from running some other program.

/DATE displays time and date at all times.

/TEXT causes the Shell to operate in text mode. If this option is not speci-fied, the Shell will come up in graphics mode as long as there is a graphics-capable display adapter present. If only a monochrome display adapter is avail-able, the Shell will automatically go into text mode even without the /TEXT instruction.

/LF adjusts the mouse for left-hand use.

/CO1 forces use of 640x350, 16-color display mode.

/CO2 forces use of 640x480, two-color display mode.

/CO3 forces use of 640x480, 16-color display mode.

/B allocates random-access memory to File System, keeping its memory de-mands to a minimum if necessary.

/COM2 accepts use of serial mouse attached to COM2 serial port.

The Main Group

When the Shell is started, it is in "Start Programs" mode. Start Programs is the heading appearing on all screens from which the user can initiate pro-grams or switch to other menus to initiate programs. Later, we will explore the other major operating mode, "File System."

The Main Group is the top-most level of menus. Initially, four choices

are available on the Main Group menu. The user selects among them by first
using the up and down arrow keys to move the reverse video bar to the desired
choice and then hitting the Enter key.

```
 10-08-88                        Start Programs                    12:21 am
   Program  Group  Exit                                          F1=Help
                                  Main Group
                   To select an item, use the up and down arrows.
                 To start a program or display a new group, press Enter.

 Command Prompt
 Change Colors
 DOS Utilities...
 File System
```

```
 F10=Actions                          Shift+F9=Command Prompt
```

Figure 1. Main Group menu of the DOS Shell.

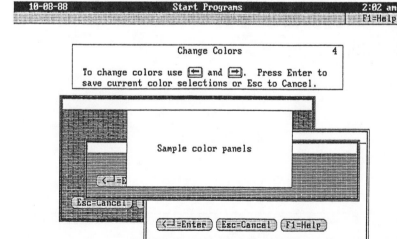

```
 10-08-88                        Start Programs                     2:02 am
                                                                  F1=Help
```

```
                          Change Colors              4

              To change colors use [←] and [→].  Press Enter to
              save current color selections or Esc to Cancel.
```

Sample color panels

```
                        [←]=Enter  [Esc=Cancel]  [F1=Help]
```

```
 [←]=Enter  Esc=Cancel
```

Figure 2. Change Colors routine of the Main Group menu.

"Command Prompt" allows the user to temporarily exit the Shell. The regular system prompt, A> or C>, appears and the user can run programs and execute DOS commands as if the Shell had never been present. When the user wishes to return to the Shell, however, all that is necessary is to type **EXIT** at the system prompt. The Shell was always there, inactive in the background, but ready to be invoked so as to return to the comfortable cocoon of a menu-based user interface.

"Change Colors" is a built-in routine that allows users who have color monitors to choose from among a variety of color combinations for the parts of the Shell. To change color combinations just strike the left and right arrow keys. Colors will change onscreen. A number in the upper right-hand corner of the box titled "Change Colors" helps keep track of where you are. The number of unique color schemes will vary with the type of color display adapter you are using.

The "DOS Utilities..." item on the Main Group menu is itself a menu. You can tell that from the ellipsis following the title of the option. To jump to the DOS Utilities menu, highlight the choice and strike Enter.

```
 10-08-88                    Start Programs                    1:50 am
 Program  Group  Exit                                         F1=Help
                          DOS Utilities...
                To select an item, use the up and down arrows.
             To start a program or display a new group, press Enter.

 Set Date and Time
 Disk Copy
 Disk Compare
 Backup Fixed Disk
 Restore Fixed Disk
 Format
 Wide Directory




 F10=Actions   Esc=Cancel   Shift+F9=Command Prompt
```

Figure 3. DOS Utilities menu within the Main Group menu.

The choices listed (see Figure 3), while useful in themselves, are designed to demonstrate how to create additional menus of DOS commands and other program options. As with any other Shell menu, the user highlights a choice, then presses the Enter key to activate it.

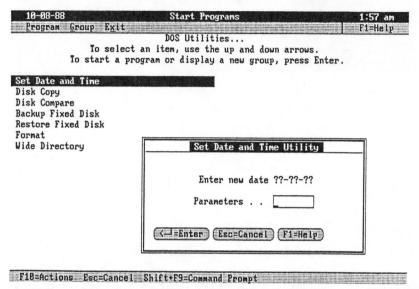

Figure 4. Set Date and Time Utility of the DOS Utilities menu.

In Figure 4, the title, prompt line, and input area are all controlled by a series of instructions stored with the Set Date and Time menu choice. After the date is filled in, a similar box appears requesting time information.

Creating and Modifying Menus

The action bar across the top of the screen, just below the Start Programs title line, is the key to modifying the menus provided with the DOS Shell. Let's go back to the Main Group menu (press Esc to move from a lower level back to a higher level menu).

To get to the action bar, press F10. Program will be highlighted. To add programs to the Main Group, as distinguished from adding groups of programs, highlight Program and press Enter. Rather than adding programs to the Main Group, however, we will start a new group, i.e., menu, containing a list of activities associated with processing information regarding overdue library materials; using the appropriate arrow key, move the highlight to Group and press the Enter key.

36   The Operating System: PC-DOS

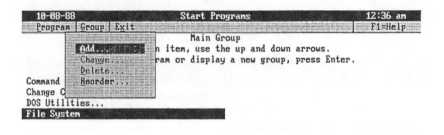

Figure 5. Using the action bar of the Main Group menu to start a new menu.

Note that Add and Reorder are in bold type, while Change and Delete are in plain. Only those choices in bold type are available. Since the File System, the highlighted menu item, isn't a group in and of itself, it can be neither changed nor deleted. If you are using the DOS Shell in character mode—rather than in the graphics mode shown throughout this discussion—asterisks in the middle of a pull-down menu choice rather than faint type will indicate that the choice is not available within the current context.

Reorder, however, applies to the currently displayed group rather than to the highlighted menu item. By selecting Reorder, it is possible to move the currently highlighted menu item, File System, up or down the list of Main Group choices. Add is also active. It is possible to add a new group to the Main Group. Indeed, that is exactly what we will do.

Highlighting Add and pressing Enter opens the Add Group box (see Figure 6). The user must enter at least a title (of a maximum of 37 characters including spaces) and a filename (of up to eight characters). The user may opt to also provide up to 478 characters of help information to be displayed when the F1 help key is pressed while the title of the new group is highlighted, and a password of up to eight characters. Only users who know the the library's OD2 password will be able to make use of the Overdues Processing menu or change that menu later. While the windows for entry of title and help text are

short, it is possible to scroll horizontally as needed. The user cycles through
the four Add Group entry areas by pressing the Enter key or the Tab key.
When everything is to the user's satisfaction, pressing F2 saves information
for the new group and adds its title to the Main Group menu list.

```
10-08-88                    Start Programs              12:44 am
  Program  Group  Exit                                    F1=Help
                          Main Group
           To select an item, use the up and down arrows.
           To start a program or display a new group, press Enter.

Command Prompt
Change Colors          ┌──────────── Add Group ────────────┐
DOS Utilities..        │
File System            │ Required
                       │
                       │   Title . . . .  │Overdues Processing│→
                       │
                       │   Filename  . .  │OVERDUES│
                       │
                       │   Optional
                       │
                       │   Help text . .  │Process overdues using│→
                       │
                       │   Password  . .  │OD2 _ │
                       │
                       │   ( Esc=Cancel ) ( F1=Help ) ( F2=Save )
                       └────────────────────────────────────┘

  F10=Actions              Shift+F9=Command Prompt
```

Figure 6. Add Group box, used to add groups to the Main group.

```
10-08-88                    Start Programs              12:50 am
  Program  Group  Exit                                    F1=Help
                          Main Group
           To select an item, use the up and down arrows.
           To start a program or display a new group, press Enter.

Command Prompt
Change Colors
DOS Utilities...
File System
Overdues Processing...




  F10=Actions              Shift+F9=Command Prompt
```

Figure 7. Main Group menu with the added group at the end of the list.

Note that Overdues Processing has been added to the end of the list of menu choices (see Figure 7). To move it to another position, press F10 to go to the action bar and select the Reorder option from the Group pull-down menu. The ellipsis after Overdues Processing reminds the user that Overdues Processing refers to another group rather than to a single program. To add programs to the Overdues Processing group, highlight that title and press Enter.

```
 10-08-88                      Start Programs                   1:15 am
  Program  Group  Exit                                         F1=Help
                             Main Group
            To select an item, use the up and down arrows.
            To start a program or display a new group, press Enter.
Comm   ┌─────────────Password──────────────────────┐
Chai   │                                            │
DOS    │   Type password then press                 │
Fil    │   Enter.                                    │
Ove    │                                            │
       │   Password . . ┌──────────┐                │
       │                └──────────┘                │
       │                                            │
       │  (←┘=Enter)  (Esc=Cancel)  (F1=Help)       │
       └────────────────────────────────────────────┘



 F10=Actions              Shift+F9=Command Prompt
```

Figure 8. Password box in which—as a security measure—the typed-in characters do not display.

Because we specified that Overdues Processing was to be protected by password, we must enter the assigned password before proceeding. As we type OD2 (the password we chose in creating the group), the cursor advances but no characters are displayed (see Figure 8). It is less likely that someone will pick up a password they should not have if it does not appear on the screen when typed.

   As shown in Figure 9, the group is indeed empty! To add programs, we press F10 to highlight the Program choice on the action bar and choose the only available option under it: adding a program.

   As soon as programs are added to the Overdues Processing group, the Start, Change, Delete, and Copy options will be active.

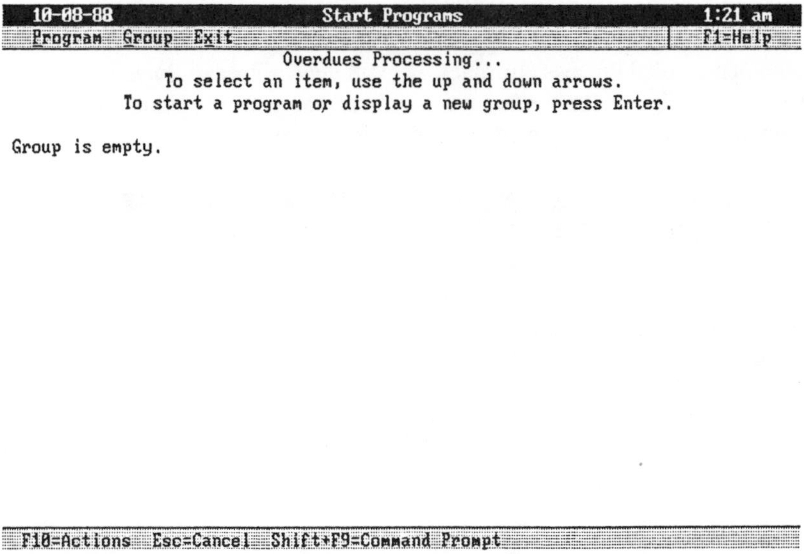

```
 10-08-88                  Start Programs              1:21 am
  Program  Group  Exit                                F1=Help
                   Overdues Processing...
          To select an item, use the up and down arrows.
         To start a program or display a new group, press Enter.

Group is empty.
```

```
 F10=Actions  Esc=Cancel  Shift+F9=Command Prompt
```

Figure 9. Password-protected Overdues Processing with "empty group" message.

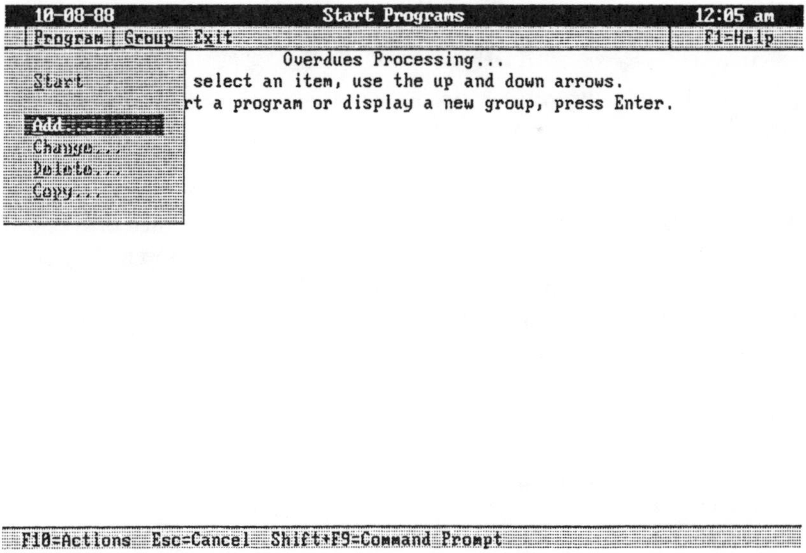

```
 10-08-88                  Start Programs             12:05 am
  Program  Group  Exit                                F1=Help
                   Overdues Processing...
  Start         select an item, use the up and down arrows.
                rt a program or display a new group, press Enter.
  Add
  Change...
  Delete
  Copy...
```

```
 F10=Actions  Esc=Cancel  Shift+F9=Command Prompt
```

Figure 10. Choosing Add to add programs to the empty Overdues Processing group.

Program Start-Up Commands

Menu items called Process Overdues, Backup Items File, and Backup Borrow-
er File have been added to the Overdues Processing group. Figure 11 shows
how you can change the Process Overdues menu item.

```
 10-08-88                    Start Programs                    1:43 am
   Program  Group  Exit                                      F1=Help
                       Overdues Processing...
              To select an item, use the up and down arrows.
           To start a program or display a new group, press Enter.

 Process Overdues
  Backup Items Fi          Change Program
  Backup Borrower
                  Required

                     Title . . . .    Process Overdues       →

                     Commands  . .    CD C:\OVERDUES||DBXL OD→

                  Optional

                     Help text . .    Main overdues processi→

                     Password  . .   OD2

                    Esc=Cancel   F1=Help   F2=Save

 F10=Actions  Esc=Cancel  Shift+F9=Command Prompt
```

*Figure 11. Overdues Processing group with three menu items added and the
Change Program box displayed.*

By far the most important portion of the Change Program and Add Program
boxes is the Commands line. The user can enter up to 500 characters of commands that will be executed whenever a given menu item is chosen. Any program name or DOS command that would be legal in a batch file can be used
here, with the exception of the **GOTO** command.

When Process Overdues is chosen from the Overdues Processing menu,
the following commands are executed:

CD C:\OVERDUES
DBXL OD

The double vertical bar (see Command line in Figure 11) is produced
with the F4 key and separates DOS commands that would normally be issued
one at a time from the DOS prompt or entered one to a line in a batch file.

With 500 characters to work with, it is possible to construct considerably more powerful menus than the one shown here.

A new set of operators is provided to give the creator of Program Start-up Commands ("new wave batch files") considerable control over the Shell's actions subsequent to selection of a given menu option. The following options must be enclosed in square brackets ([ ]) in order to perform properly:

/T "title": Defines a title for the window that appears when the corresponding program is chosen from a group menu. Maximum of 40 characters.

/I "instructions": Specifies up to 40 characters of instructions displayed for user within prompt window.

/P "prompt message": Wording of prompting label on same line as entry field in window. Maximum of 20 characters.

/F "drive:\path\filename": Prompts for drive, path, and filename and checks to be sure they exist before proceeding further. Up to 76 characters are allowed.

%n: Saves a value entered when a routine is started for later use. The %n must be the first element inside the square brackets for its value to be set aside for subsequent use. Allowable values of n are zero through nine.

/C "%n": Defines the value of %n for a subsequent task as the same as the value of %n from a previous task. Allowable values of n are 0 through 9.

/D "default value": Shows a default value in entry field. It can be over-typed. Maximum of 40 characters.

/D "%n": Shows as a default value in the entry field the value for %n previously defined by a /C "%n" option. Allowable values of n are 0 through 9.

/R: Clears the default value shown in the entry area of the prompt box after the first key press.

/L "number of characters in entry field": Specifies allowable length of entry field, up to 127 characters.

/M "e": Allows entry only of filenames that already exist.

Several other operators are available as well. They must not be enclosed in square brackets, however:

%n: Without the brackets, %n serves the same purpose in a collection of program startup commands as it does in a batch file. It passes up to ten values specified on the command line to the programs that follow.

/#: Substitutes the drive letter of the drive from which the Shell was started and a colon into the program startup commands.

/@: Substitutes the path from the root directory of the drive from which the Shell was started into the program startup commands.

If a batch file is to be called from within a group of program startup commands, the **CALL** command should be used. Without it, control will not return to the Shell when the called batch file comes to an end.

The File System

The File System replaces a variety of disparate, stand-alone file-management commands. While many of the less frequently used options are not represented

```
 10-08-88                    File System                      2:09 am
 File  Options  Arrange  Exit                                 F1=Help
  Ctrl+letter selects a drive.
  A   B   C

  B:\
        Directory Tree                        *.*

 √B:\                             COMP     .COM      9,491   06-17-88
                                  DEBUG    .COM     21,606   06-17-88
                                  DISKCOMP .COM      9,889   06-17-88
                                  DOS01L   .400          0   06-17-88
                                  DOSUTIL  .MEU      6,660   06-17-88
                                  EDLIN    .COM     14,249   06-17-88
                                  FILESYS  .EXE     11,125   06-17-88
                                  FIND     .EXE      5,983   06-17-88
                                  FORMAT   .COM     22,923   06-17-88
                                  GRAFTABL .COM     18,271   06-17-88
                                  GRAPHICS .COM     16,733   06-17-88
                                  GRAPHICS .PRO      9,413   06-17-88
                                  JOIN     .EXE     17,457   06-17-88
                                  LABEL    .COM      4,490   06-17-88
                                  MEM      .EXE     20,133   06-17-88
                                  MORE     .COM      2,166   06-17-88
 F10=Actions  Shift+F9=Command Prompt
```

Figure 12. The File System screen, showing a list of files with the active file specification and scroll bar, and the directory tree of the currently logged disk drive.

in the file system, most beginning users will find the tools provided by the File System more than adequate for carrying on routine "housekeeping" chores.

In Figure 12, the right half of the screen is occupied by a list of the files on the currently specified disk drive and directory. The currently active file specification ("*.*" in this instance) is shown just above the list of files. It is possible to change this specification so as to show only files matching certain criteria for filename and filename extension, as we will see shortly.

The scroll bar on the right edge of the screen indicates how many undisplayed files are above and below those currently visible. If a mouse is active, the screen window can be scrolled by pointing at either end of the scroll bar and clicking. The arrow keys and PgUp and PgDn keys are also operative. If you are using the Shell in character rather than graphics mode, the screen display will look slightly different (e.g., a symbol will be placed next to a filename only when it is selected) and you will not be able to use a mouse. An arrow will indicate that there are more files to be found by scrolling using the arrow, PgUp, and PgDn keys.

Also in Figure 12, the symbol to the left of each filename indicates whether a given file is executable (.COM, .EXE, and .BAT filename extensions) or non-executable and presumed to be text. Executable files can be run by placing the highlight over the filename and hitting the Enter key, by selecting the file and using the Open option from the File pull-down menu, or by double-clicking on the filename with a mouse (if you've got one).

The left half of the screen shows the directory tree of the currently logged disk drive. You can move among the files area on the right, the directory area on the left, the action bar at the top of the screen, and the drive-select area just below it by using the Tab key.

On a hard disk drive, a large number of directories can be displayed in the directory area. The user can move among them with the arrow keys and select a new default directory by highlighting its name and pressing Enter. The files window will change to show the contents of the newly chosen directory.

In Figure 13, the first choice on the action bar is File. Its pull-down menu includes a variety of common operations. Most of them are not active, however, until one or more files have been selected. To select a file, move to the files window, using the Tab key. Highlight the file(s) of interest, then press the space bar. In the graphics mode, the symbol to the left of the file

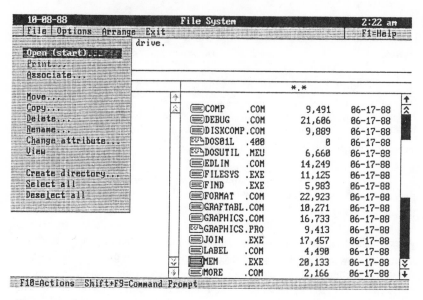

Figure 13. Selections under the File choice of File System's action bar (left); in the files list (right), MEM.EXE has been selected, as is evident by the high-lighted symbol.

name will turn color to indicate the file has been selected; in character mode, a symbol is placed next to the filename only when it is selected.

Most of the choices on this pull-down are direct substitutes for or improvements upon the most common versions of existing stand-alone DOS commands:

DOS Shell	DOS
Open	(type filename)
Print	PRINT
Associate	[no equivalent]
Move	COPY, then DELETE
Copy	COPY
Delete	DEL
Rename	REN
Change attribute	ATTRIB
View	TYPE
Create directory	CHDIR
Select all	[no equivalent]
Deselect all	[no equivalent]

Notice that Print is faint (see Figure 13), indicating that it is unavailable within the current context. That makes sense, as the only selected file is MEM.EXE, a program file rather than a text file. If we were to select DOSUTIL.MEU or some other text file, Print would be in bold, but Open (start) would be unavailable.

Let's explore a number of the File menu options.

The Open File option prompts for optional parameters before running the specified program. Options might include a drive letter, one or more filenames, or various switch values depending on what is expected and can be used by the program that is being invoked. A program must be selected before it can be opened.

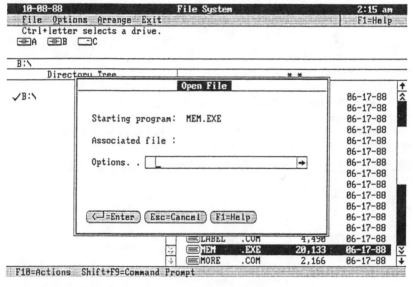

Figure 14. The Open File option of File System's File menu.

The Associate File concept is genuinely new for DOS. It is designed to automatically invoke a particular program whenever a file with a specified filename extension is opened. In the example in Figure 15, choosing a file ending with .EXE or .TXT will automatically invoke the **FIND** command. A more practical use than the one depicted might be the association of FOXPLUS, the filename for the Foxbase Plus database-management system, with the .PRG filename extension. It is then a one-step process to load Foxbase and run a given Foxbase program by opening the appropriate file.

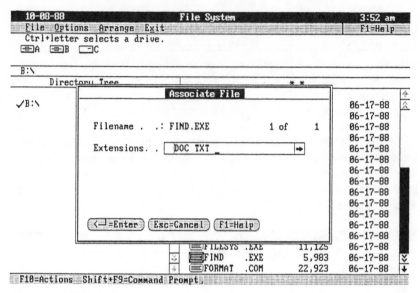

Figure 15. The Associate File Option.

No more than 20 filename extensions in total can be associated with a program or programs. That means that 20 extensions can be associated with one program, 10 extensions can be associated with each of two programs, or one extension can be associated with each of 20 programs.

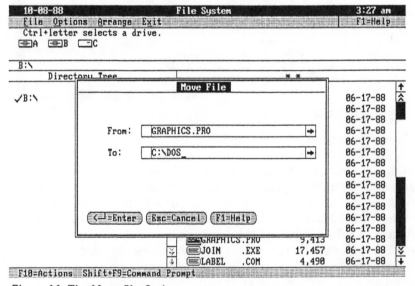

Figure 16. The Move file Option.

The Move File option is pretty straightforward (see Figure 16). You just specify the new drive and directory path and the Shell transfers the file to the new location and deletes references to it at the old location.

Change Attribute indicates, by way of a pointer symbol, which of the three possible file attributes are turned on (see Figure 17). The fourth file attribute—the System attribute—cannot be changed from within the Shell. If you are finally getting down to systematizing backup of files on your hard disk and wish to turn the archive attribute of a large number of them off, Change Attribute, in combination with the display options to be discussed later, can be of great help.

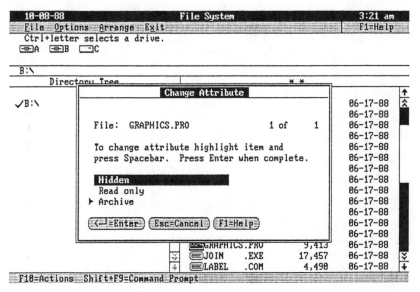

Figure 17. The Change Attribute Option.

Files can be hidden—they won't appear when you type DIR—but they will still be visible from within the File System. The Read-Only option (see Change Attribute box in Figure 17) makes it impossible for the user to delete, rename, or overwrite the current version of a file. Setting the read-only option on can add security in some situations where many people are using the same computer and accidental erasure and overwriting are possibilities.

View is a major improvement over "dumb old" **TYPE**. You can page through a text file a screen at a time and browse backward as well as forward. In Figure 18, the contents of the GRAPHICS.PRO text file, a collection of

information about printers used in conjunction with the **GRAPHICS** command, is shown.

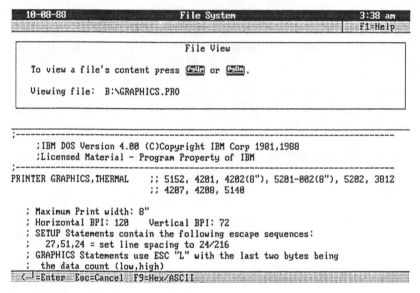

Figure 18. The View Option.

Advanced users may from time to time wish to examine a program file.
The F9 key switches between a text format display (ASCII) and a display of
the contents of the program file in hexadecimal format (see Figure 19). Generally speaking, if you know why this might be useful, you'll be happy to see
it in the DOS Shell. If you haven't a clue as to what use it might have, for
you it has no importance.

To create a new subdirectory, just choose the Create Directory option
from the File pull-down menu and fill in the blank (see Figure 20).

It is sometimes helpful to be able to select all the files in the current
subdirectory, and to subsequently deselect all of them. If you wish to Move,
Copy, Delete, Rename, or Change the attribute of most (but not all) of the
files in a directory, it is faster to Select all (see Figure 21), then use the space
bar to deselect the few that should be left out of subsequent operations. Note
that View is not available if more than one file is selected.

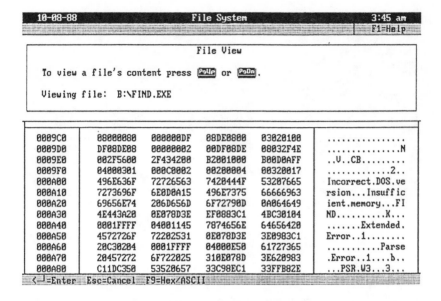

Figure 19. A display of the contents of B:\FIND.EXE in hexadecimal format.

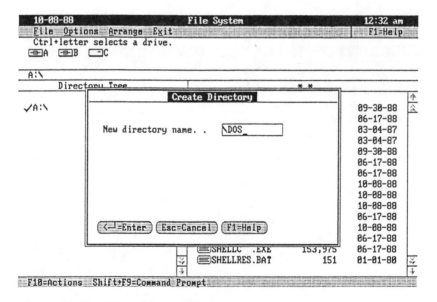

Figure 20. The Create Directory Option.

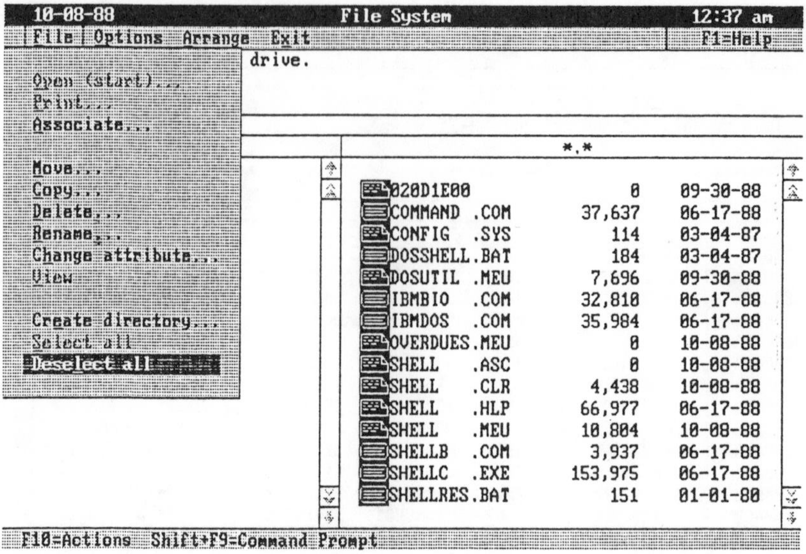

Figure 21. The current subdirectory with all files selected and Deselect All high-lighted; note View is unavailable.

Options

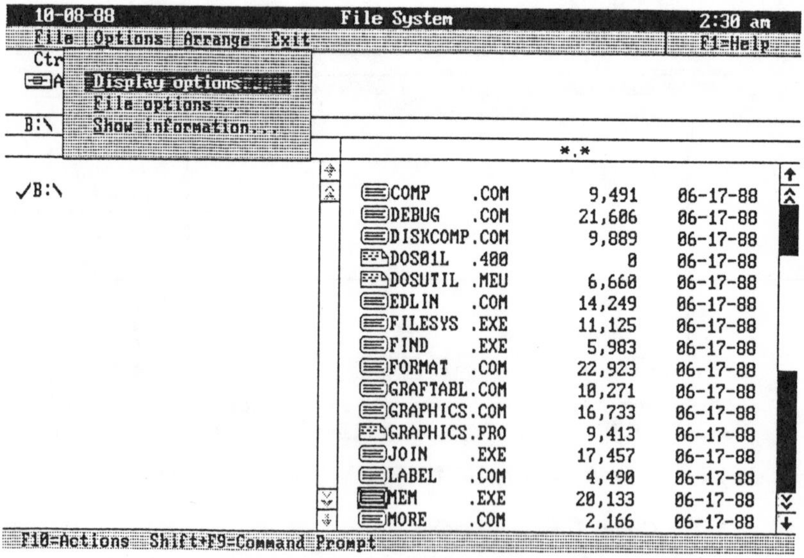

Figure 22. The pull-down menu of the Options item on File System's action bar.

The Options item on the File System action bar offers three choices. The most powerful is Display Options.

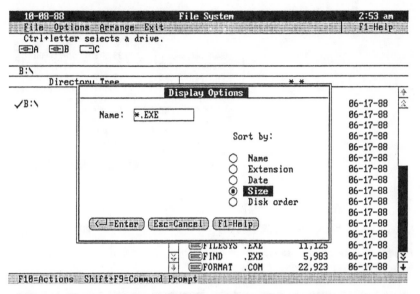

Figure 23. The Display Options choice through which the user can change the filenames and the sort order in which they are presented.

By changing the Name (see Figure 23), it is possible to display only a portion of the files present in the current directory. The "*" and "?" wildcards can be used to substitute for several characters or one character, respectively. To view only the files ending in .EXE, we specify a Name of *.EXE. When you first enter the File System, *.* is the default file specification.

Irrespective of whether changes are made to the Name, changes can be made to the sort order in which filenames are presented. All five possible sort orders have their uses. Disk order (see Figure 23), for example, refers to the physical order of the files on disk.

Notice that, in Figure 24, the new filename specification (*.EXE) is displayed directly above the list of filenames. A sort by size can make it much easier to weed out large and unnecessary files when your disk begins to approach capacity.

File Options control whether you will be asked to confirm file deletions and the replacement of one file by another during copy operations.

```
 10-08-88                    File System                    2:59 am
  File  Options  Arrange  Exit                             F1=Help
  Ctrl+letter selects a drive.
  =A  =B  =C
 ─────────────────────────────────────────────────────────────────
  B:\
 ──────────────────────────┬──────────────────────────────────────
      Directory Tree        │                *.EXE
                            │
  √B:\                      │   SHELLC  .EXE    153,975    06-17-88
                            │   MEM     .EXE     20,133    06-17-88
                            │   ATTRIB  .EXE     18,247    06-17-88
                            │   SUBST   .EXE     18,143    06-17-88
                            │   JOIN    .EXE     17,457    06-17-88
                            │   REPLACE .EXE     17,199    06-17-88
                            │   APPEND  .EXE     11,170    06-17-88
                            │   FILESYS .EXE     11,125    06-17-88
                            │   NLSFUNC .EXE      6,910    06-17-88
                            │   FIND    .EXE      5,983    06-17-88
                            │   SORT    .EXE      5,914    06-17-88
 ─────────────────────────────────────────────────────────────────
  F10=Actions  Shift+F9=Command Prompt
```

Figure 24. The current subdirectory with SORT highlighted; note the new file-name specification displayed above the list.

```
 10-08-88                    File System                    3:14 am
  File  Options  Arrange  Exit                             F1=Help
  Ctrl+letter selects a drive.
  =A  =B  =C
 ─────────────────────────────────────────────────────────────────
  B:┌──────  File Options  ──────┐
    │                            │              *.*
    │                            │
  √B│ ⊠ Confirm on delete      D .EXE     11,170    06-17-88
    │ ⊠ Confirm on replace     N .COM      5,785    06-17-88
    │ □ Select across directories B .EXE   18,247    06-17-88
    │                          P .COM     33,754    06-17-88
    │                            .COM      1,065    06-17-88
    │                          A .COM     36,285    06-17-88
    │ (⏎=Enter) (Esc=Cancel) (F1=Help) K .COM  17,771  06-17-88
    └────────────────────────────┘ .COM    9,491    06-17-88
                            │   DEBUG   .COM     21,606    06-17-88
                            │   DISKCOMP.COM      9,889    06-17-88
                            │   DOS01L  .400          0    06-17-88
                            │   DOSUTIL .MEU      6,660    06-17-88
                            │   EDLIN   .COM     14,249    06-17-88
                            │   FILESYS .EXE     11,125    06-17-88
                            │   FIND    .EXE      5,983    06-17-88
                            │   FORMAT  .COM     22,923    06-17-88
 ─────────────────────────────────────────────────────────────────
  F10=Actions  Shift+F9=Command Prompt
```

Figure 25. The File Options box displays confirmation requests.

The default, as indicated in Figure 25, is to prompt for user approval. This setting can be changed by highlighting the option and pressing the Enter key.

The Select Across Directories item determines whether the Shell will allow you to select files in several directories in order to eventually perform a File operation on them. If this option is turned off, as it is in Figure 25, all selected files will be automatically deselected when the user moves to a new directory. For statistics such as name of file and size of directory, choose the Show Information Option (see Figure 26).

```
10-08-88                        File System                      1:08 am
  File  Options  Arrange  Exit                                 F1=Help
 Ctr┌──────────────────────────────┐
 ⌐▣A│    Show Information           │
    │                              │
    │ File                         │
 A:\│   Name  : COMMAND.COM         │
    │   Attr  : ...a               │            *.*
 ───│ Selected        A            ├──────────────────────────────────
    │   Number:       3            │ 020D1E00          0      09-30-88
 √A:\│  Size  :   106,431          │COMMAND .COM   37,637      06-17-88
    │ Directory                    │CONFIG  .SYS      114      03-04-87
    │   Name  : ROOT               │DOSSHELL.BAT      184      03-04-87
    │   Size  :   354,707          │DOSUTIL .MEU    7,696      09-30-88
    │   Files :      15            │IBMBIO  .COM   32,810      06-17-88
    │ Disk                         │IBMDOS  .COM   35,984      06-17-88
    │   Name  :                    │OVERDUES.MEU        0      10-08-88
    │   Size  :   362,496          │SHELL   .ASC        0      10-08-88
    │   Avail :       0            │SHELL   .CLR    4,438      10-08-88
    │   Files :      15            │SHELL   .HLP   66,977      06-17-88
    │   Dirs  :       1            │SHELL   .MEU   10,004      10-08-88
    │                              │SHELLB  .COM    3,937      06-17-88
    │ [Esc=Cancel]  [F1=Help]      │SHELLC  .EXE  153,975      06-17-88
    └──────────────────────────────┘SHELLRES.BAT      151      01-01-80
  F10=Actions  Shift+F9=Command Prompt
```

Figure 26. The Show Information choice from the Options pull-down menu gives detailed statistics on a disk, directory, and file group.

Arrange

In the pull-down menu of Arrange, System File List provides another way of viewing statistics on the files in the current directory.

Unlike Show Information from the Options menu, System File List provides a constant and dynamic report on the count and size of files. If navigation among a variety of directories is not generally necessary, using the System File List format may be preferable to displaying the directory tree.

Unfortunately, System File List and Multiple File List are mutually exclusive. If you wish to view the contents of two directories, you will have to get by with the Show Information approach.

```
 10-08-88                        File System                      12:26 am
 File  Options  Arrange  Exit                                      F1=Help
  Ctrl+letter
  ▭A   ▭B  ┌──────────────────────┐
          │  Single file list     │
          │  Multiple file list   │
  A:\     │  System file list     │
          └──────────────────────┘
       Directo                                        *.*
                            ▒020D1E00            0     09-30-88
  ✓A:\                       COMMAND .COM    37,637   06-17-88
                             CONFIG  .SYS       114   03-04-87
                             DOSSHELL.BAT       184   03-04-87
                             DOSUTIL .MEU     7,696   09-30-88
                             IBMBIO  .COM    32,810   06-17-88
                             IBMDOS  .COM    35,984   06-17-88
                             OVERDUES.MEU         0   10-08-88
                             SHELL   .ASC         0   10-08-88
                             SHELL   .CLR     4,438   10-08-88
                             SHELL   .HLP    66,977   06-17-88
                             SHELL   .MEU    10,804   10-08-88
                             SHELLB  .COM     3,937   06-17-88
                             SHELLC  .EXE   153,975   06-17-88
                             SHELLRES.BAT       151   01-01-80
 F10=Actions  Shift+F9=Command Prompt
```

Figure 27. The pull-down menu of the Arrange item on File System's action bar.

```
 10-08-88                        File System                       2:47 am
 File  Options  Arrange  Exit                                      F1=Help
  Ctrl+letter selects a drive.
  ▭A   ▭B  ▭C

  B:\
                                                    *.*
 File
   Name : MORTGAGE.BAS        FORMAT  .COM    22,923   06-17-88  12:00pm
   Attr :  ...a               GRAFTABL.COM    10,271   06-17-88  12:00pm
 Selected     B    A          GRAPHICS.COM    16,733   06-17-88  12:00pm
   Number:    3    0          GRAPHICS.PRO     9,413   06-17-88  12:00pm
   Size :    2,057            JOIN    .EXE    17,457   06-17-88  12:00pm
 Directory                    LABEL   .COM     4,490   06-17-88  12:00pm
   Name : ROOT                MEM     .EXE    20,133   06-17-88  12:00pm
   Size :  668,270            MORE    .COM     2,166   06-17-88  12:00pm
   Files :      40            MORTGAGE.BAS     6,207   06-17-88  12:00pm
 Disk                         NLSFUNC .EXE     6,910   06-17-88  12:00pm
   Name :                     PCIBMDRV.MOS       295   06-17-88  12:00pm
   Size :  728,064            PCMSDRV .MOS       961   06-17-88  12:00pm
   Avail :  50,688            PCMSPDRV.MOS       801   06-17-88  12:00pm
   Files :      40            PRINT   .COM    14,163   06-17-88  12:00pm
   Dirs :       1             RECOVER .COM    10,732   06-17-88  12:00pm
 F10=Actions  Shift+F9=Command Prompt
```

Figure 28. System File List provides a constant and dynamic report on the count and size of files.

```
 10-08-88                    File System                  12:21 am
 File  Options  Arrange  Exit                             F1=Help
 Ctrl+letter selects a drive.
 ⊜A   ⊜B   ⊏⊐C

 B:\
            Directory Tree                    *.*
 ✓B:\                            ⬆
                                 ⌃   ▦FILESYS .EXE     11,125   06-17-88   ⬆
                                     ▦FIND    .EXE      5,983   06-17-88   ⌃
                                     ▦FORMAT  .COM     22,923   06-17-88   ▮
                                     ▦GRAFTABL.COM     10,271   06-17-88   ⌄
                                 ⌄   ▦GRAPHICS.COM     16,733   06-17-88   ⬇
                                 ⬇

 ⊜A   ⊜B   ⊏⊐C

            Directory Tree                    *.*
 ✓A:\                            ⬆
                                 ⌃   ▦SHELL   .MEU      5,624   09-30-88   ⬆
                                     ▦SHELLB  .COM      3,937   06-17-88   ⌃
                                     ▦SHELLC  .EXE    153,975   06-17-88   ▮
                                     ▦SHELLRES.BAT        151   01-01-80   ⌄
                                 ⌄   ▦SHELLTRA.BAT        156   09-30-88   ⬇
                                 ⬇
 F10=Actions  Shift+F9=Command Prompt
```

Figure 29. Dual-directory display capacity.

The Tab key is used to navigate from one directory to the next, and within each directory from the directory tree display to the files display. While comparison of the contents of one directory with those of another is one of the obvious applications of a dual-directory display capacity (see Figure 29), the purpose would have been better served by an approach that divided the screen vertically rather than horizontally and reduced the amount of space allocated for the directory tree.

Display options can be used to change the file specification that determines what files will be displayed (see Figure 30). There is no way to create separate specifications for each directory, however.

When you are done, use the Exit choice of File System's action bar (exit by pressing the specified function key) to return to the Main Group menu.

Help

The key to press for Help is constantly displayed in the far right-hand corner of File System's action bar; wherever you are in the DOS Shell, help messages are available by pressing the F1 key.

```
 10-08-88                       File System                       3:07 am
  File  Options  Arrange  Exit                              F1=Help
  Ctrl+letter selects a drive.
  ⊟A   ⊟B   ⊡C

 B:\
              Directory Tree                          *.COM
 √B:\                                 ⊕
                                      ⊼   ⊟ASSIGN   .COM     5,785   06-17-88  ⊼
                                          ⊟BACKUP   .COM    33,754   06-17-88
                                          ⊟BASIC    .COM     1,065   06-17-88
                                      ⊻   ⊟BASICA   .COM    36,285   06-17-88  ⊻
                                      ↓   ⊟CHKDSK   .COM    17,771   06-17-88  ↓


  ⊟A   ⊟B   ⊡C


              Directory Tree                          *.COM
 √A:\                                 ⊕
                                      ⊼   ⊟COMMAND  .COM    37,637   06-17-88  ⊼
                                          ⊟IBMBIO   .COM    32,810   06-17-88
                                          ⊟IBMDOS   .COM    35,984   06-17-88
                                      ⊻   ⊟SHELLB   .COM     3,937   06-17-88  ⊻
                                      ↓
  F10=Actions  Shift+F9=Command Prompt
```

Figure 30. Dual-directory display with changed file specifications (*.COM above both lists).

```
 10-08-88                       File System                       4:30 am
  File  Options  Arrange  Exit                              F1=Help
  Ctrl+letter selects a
  ⊟A   ⊟B   ⊡C          Exit File System      F3
                        Resume File System
 B:\
              Directory Tree                          *.*
 √B:\                                 ⊕
                                      ⊼   ⊟APPEND    .EXE    11,170   06-17-88  ⊼
                                          ⊟ASSIGN    .COM     5,785   06-17-88
                                          ⊟ATTRIB    .EXE    18,247   06-17-88
                                          ⊟BACKUP    .COM    33,754   06-17-88
                                          ⊟BASIC     .COM     1,065   06-17-88
                                          ⊟BASICA    .COM    36,285   06-17-88
                                          ⊟CHKDSK    .COM    17,771   06-17-88
                                          ⊟COMP      .COM     9,491   06-17-88
                                          ⊟DEBUG     .COM    21,606   06-17-88
                                          ⊟DISKCOMP.COM       9,889   06-17-88
                                          ⊟DOS01L    .400         0   06-17-88
                                          ⊟DOSUTIL   .MEU     6,660   06-17-88
                                          ⊟EDLIN     .COM    14,249   06-17-88
                                          ⊟FILESYS   .EXE    11,125   06-17-88
                                      ⊻   ⊟FIND      .EXE     5,983   06-17-88  ⊻
                                      ↓   ⊟FORMAT    .COM    22,923   06-17-88  ↓
  F10=Actions  Shift+F9=Command Prompt
```

Figure 31. Selecting Exit File System to return to the Main Group menu.

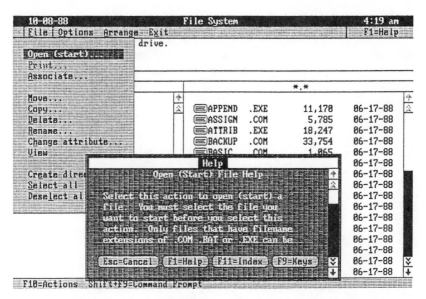

Figure 32. The Help box is available at all times simply by pressing F1.

Help messages are context-sensitive, offering information appropriate to the context at hand. The arrow keys allow you to scroll through the file. Pressing F11 will bring up a list of the other help messages contained in the Shell. You can select and read any message in the system. If your keyboard has no F11 key, an Alt-F1 key combination has the same effect. Pressing F9 displays a list of special key functions. Since the currently available special keys and their meanings are usually shown at the bottom of the screen, it is not often necessary to refer to them in the help system.

Observations

The specifications, features, and operation of the DOS Shell are likely to change significantly from version to version of DOS. Such systems tend to evolve quickly in response to user demands and competition from other vendors in the field. This section can only describe the Shell as it is in version 4.0.

It is likely that public-domain software libraries will begin to collect fancy menu systems contrived with the new DOS Shell program startup commands.

Users will get used to the ease of learning that the Shell offers. Perhaps the example of the Shell will move users more quickly into the graphically-oriented OS/2, the sophisticated and expensive "operating system of the future" developed by Microsoft and IBM. On the other hand, the DOS Shell may remove most of the ease-of-use justification for considering a move to OS/2. If DOS is just as easy, and much less expensive, why bother?

4

USEFUL DOS COMMANDS AND CONCEPTS

We've covered the commands that just about every user of an IBM PC-compatible computer needs to understand. Here we will look at some DOS commands and concepts that, while less critical, can be extremely helpful in many circumstances.

Keep in mind that some options, and a limited number of commands, are not available in earlier versions of DOS. Further, some manufacturers customize DOS in highly proprietary ways. AT&T, for instance, includes a **HELP** command in the version of DOS it supplies with certain of its computers.

These "useful" DOS facilities are treated by group: Configuring the System, Hard Disk Management, Filters and Pipes, and Miscellaneous.

Configuring the System

DOS provides a framework within which applications programs can function. Fortunately, the framework is flexible, allowing users to make adjustments for the peculiar requirements of a wide variety of specific applications programs. The keys to that flexibility are the DOS commands discussed in this section, and two very special disk files. The files are CONFIG.SYS and AUTOEXEC.BAT. Every time the system is booted, DOS looks for them on the default disk drive. If they are found, their contents are executed. If they are absent, the boot process continues using default values for the DOS parameters open to customization.

The commands found in CONFIG.SYS take the form of assignment statements. You can specify the number of buffers and files with which you want to operate. Device drivers are installed here; these are software routines that enable DOS to work with devices that it would otherwise not be able to handle. The number of installed disk drives can be indicated as well.

AUTOEXEC.BAT is a batch file. It is unique because of its name. DOS will execute the contents of an AUTOEXEC.BAT batch file whenever it finds one during the boot process. The user can, among other things, change the system prompt, modify settings for the screen and serial port, and set up DOS to properly print screen graphics on a printer. In fact, AUTOEXEC.BAT can contain instructions to automatically load and execute any number of programs without the user having to take any action. See the "Batch Files" chapter for information on how to create a batch file and further examples of what might appear in an AUTOEXEC.BAT batch file.

BUFFERS
Sets Buffers for Disk Access

SYNTAX: BUFFERS=<number of buffers> [,number of look-ahead buffers] [/X]

PURPOSE: Tells DOS to use more, or fewer, buffers to store data coming from and going to the disk drives. Many software packages perform more efficiently when provided with an optimum number of buffers. (Internal)

SWITCHES: / X Use expanded memory for buffer storage.

USAGE: Each buffer absorbs 532 bytes of memory. From 0 to 99 buffers may be specified if you are using DOS 3.3 or lower. With version 4.0 the limit jumped to 10,000 (provided sufficient random-access memory is present). A point of diminishing returns specific to a given program is reached beyond which additional buffers retard rather than speed up an application. A typical buffers setting is: **BUFFERS=20.**

Failing a reliable recommendation from the software publisher, trial and error is the only method for determining what **BUFFERS** setting best expedites the tasks you normally perform using your computer.

Look-ahead buffers are areas of memory into which additional sectors of disk information, located immediately after those requested by the applications program, are automatically transferred when data are retrieved from disk. In situations where the contents of a large file are retrieved in sequential order— generation of mailing labels for instance—look-ahead buffers can speed up program operation considerably.

Look-ahead buffers are set to 0 by default. Up to eight of the 512 byte memory segments can be specified in the following form: **BUF-FERS=50,5** /X. This line in a CONFIG.SYS file will result in 50 memory buffers located in expanded memory (the /X switch) and five look-ahead buffers. Look-ahead buffers are always placed in regular memory.

FILES
Selects Number of Open Files Allowed

SYNTAX: FILES=<number of open files allowed)

PURPOSE: Specifies that DOS should be ready to support up to the indicated maximum number of simultaneously open files. (Internal)

USAGE: Provision for each open file beyond the default of 8 subtracts 64 bytes from the random-access memory available to the rest of the system. You can specify from 1 to 99 open files prior to DOS 4.0 and from 8 to 255 in DOS 4.0. A common FILES statement is: **FILES=20**.

DEVICE
Installs a Device Driver

SYNTAX: DEVICE=<device driver filename>

PURPOSE: Incorporates the software routines of one or more installable device drivers into DOS as the system is booted. (Internal)

DEVICE DRIVERS: It seems like every new version of DOS is accompanied by one or two additional device drivers not included with the previous version. Here are the device drivers provided with DOS 4.0:

ANSI.SYS:	Enhances DOS facilities for screen manipulation. Required by some applications programs that take advantage of it.
DISPLAY.SYS:	Enables code page switching on an EGA or PC Convertible. DRIVER.SYS: Supports attachment of external disk drives.
PRINTER.SYS:	Supports code page switching for text and graphics output to certain IBM Proprinter and Quietwriter printers.
VDISK.SYS:	Creates an electronic imitation of a floppy disk drive using random-access memory.
XMAEM.SYS:	Supports use of extended memory as expanded memory in 80386-based computers. (DOS 4.0)
XMA2EMS.SYS:	Supports the Lotus-Intel-Microsoft (LIM) expanded memory specification, version 4. (DOS 4.0)

USAGE: Among the device drivers you might want to install are those that support CD-ROM, enhanced screen-handling facilities needed by some applications programs, and a virtual disk drive. They are installed, respectively, by the following **DEVICE** assignments:

> **DEVICE=\DEV\HITACHI.SYS   /D:MSCD000   /N:1**
> **DEVICE=ANSI.SYS**
> **DEVICE=\DOS\VDISK   100**

The named device drivers must be in the current default directory or be preceded by the appropriate pathname so that DOS can find the files when they are needed.

VDISK with the /X switch uses expanded memory for the virtual disk. The /E switch allows use of extended memory for the same purpose. As the allowable options for VDISK are highly specific to the version of DOS you have, check your DOS manual for the details.

LASTDRIVE
Highest Allowable Drive Letter

SYNTAX: LASTDRIVE=<drive letter>

PURPOSE: Sets a limit on the number of drives that can be defined by SUBST and other programs that create virtual and local drives. (Internal)

USAGE: LASTDRIVE explicitly allows use of drive designators up to a specified maximum number of logical drives for use with CD-ROM software. It is also used in conjunction with some local-area networks and serial LAN hook-ups that allow the user of one machine to access drives on another using drive letters greater than any previously assigned to the user's local system. Microsoft Extensions, discussed in the "Supplementing DOS" chapter, automatically installs the following line in CONFIG.SYS: **LASTDRIVE=Z.**

PROMPT
Changes the DOS Prompt

SYNTAX: PROMPT [new prompt string | meta-strings]

PURPOSE: Changes the system prompt. Can be used to include the current default directory path in the prompt, aiding navigation of hard disk directories. (Internal)

META-STRINGS: A number of key combinations called Meta-Strings have special meaning when combined with the **PROMPT** command. Meta-Strings always begin with a dollar-sign and are entered in lowercase. Valid Meta-Strings include:

$d	Date
$_	Carriage return and line feed
$p	Current default drive and directory
$t	Time
$g	The ">" character
$l	The "<" character
$$	The "$" character
$q	The "=" character
$b	The "|" character
$h	Backspace over the previous character
$e	Escape character

USAGE: PROMPT is often included in the AUTOEXEC.BAT file in order to change the default A> or C> with a prompt that is more informative. Hard disk users should be sure to change the prompt to something that indicates what subdirectory is the current default directory. **PROMPT** without a prompt string or Meta-String returns the prompt to its default value. Note that spaces are significant. You will usually want to add a space after the last prompt string character so that the cursor starts out one space beyond the end of the new system prompt.

   PROMPT with the $e Meta-String can be used to redefine the keyboard and move the cursor around the screen. If you have a stomach for such magic, you will find more information in the "DOS Tips and Tricks" chapter. Here are some **PROMPT** commands and the system prompt they create, assuming that we are in the \DOS subdirectory of drive C:

   C> PROMPT I am at your service oh wise librarian
   I am at your service oh wise librarian

   C> PROMPT p_$g
   C:\DOS
      >

C> PROMPT Ready pg
Ready C:\DOS>

C> PROMPT thhhhh$_$p$g

9:55
C:\DOS>

INSTALL
Installs Memory-Resident Programs

SYNTAX: INSTALL=<memory-resident program filespec>

PURPOSE: Provides a better way of installing terminate-and-stay-resident utilities than is afforded by AUTOEXEC.BAT loading. (Internal) (DOS 4.0)

USAGE: To install the FASTOPEN utility, CONFIG.SYS might include the line:

INSTALL=C:\DOS\FASTOPEN.EXE   C:=(50,25)

The parameters following the program name are those of FASTOPEN, not INSTALL. Consult the documentation that accompanies any memory-resident programs you may acquire for suggestions on whether and how to use IN-STALL.

MODE
Adjusts Screen, Printer, Port Behavior

SYNTAX: (1) **MODE** <display format> [,number of lines per screen]
           (2) **MODE** <port name and port speed>[,parity [,data bits,
               [,stop bits [,P]]]]
           (3) **MODE** <printer port>[,line width][,lines per vertical inch
               [,P]]
           (4) **MODE** <printer port> = <communications port>
           (5) **MODE** <device> <COLS=n I LINES=n>
           (6) **MODE** CON RATE=n DELAY=n
           (7) **MODE** <device> CP <PREP= I SELECT= I /STATUS
               IREFRESH
           (8) **MODE** COMx BAUD=n [PARITY= I DATA= I STOP= I
               RETRY=]

PURPOSE: (1) Specifies display format and color; (2) specifies which communications port will be used and at what speed; (3) specifies line width and vertical spacing of characters sent to a designated parallel printer port; (4) redirects printer output from a specified parallel printer port to a specified serial communications port; (5) is an alternative means of specifying number of columns and lines for printer or screen; (6) specifies number of key repetitions per second when a key is held down and the delay before repetition of a character begins; (7) sets code page parameters; and (8) is an alternative means of specifying communications port parameters. (External)

USAGE: (1) Format designation can include any of the following: 40, 80, CO40, CO80, BW40, BW80, and MONO. MONO activates the IBM-compatible monochrome display adapter. All the other designations switch to the color/graphics adapter in indicated format and color. Allowable alternatives for lines per screen are 25, 45, and 50, provided they are supported by the display adapter in use.

As soon as the **MODE** command is invoked, DOS starts using the indicated display adapter. It is not possible to drive two monitors simultaneously directly from the computer; you could contrive a Y-splitter cable approach to sending a color signal to more than one monitor, subject to considerations of signal strength. To use a color display in 80-across format, use: **MODE CO80**.

(2) DOS versions through 3.2 support only COM1 and COM2 communications ports. More recent versions also recognize COM3 and COM4. To set up COM2 to operate at 2400 bits per second with seven data bits, even parity, and one stop bit: **MODE com1:2400,e,7,1**.

The P parameter directs the computer to continuously retry if a busy signal is received. The following speeds, in bits per second, are allowed: 110, 300, 600, 1200, 2400, 4800, 9600, and—beginning with DOS 3.3—19,200. Most users rarely will need to use this option of **MODE** as communications software generally performs this kind of initialization automatically.

(3) Allowable values for line width are 80 and 132. Those for lines per inch are six and eight. The P parameter causes DOS to continuously retry a busy printer. You can direct that the printer attached to the parallel port designated as LPT1 print 132 characters per line and eight lines per inch, with automatic retry if the printer is busy: **MODE LPT1:132,8,p**. This version of the **MODE** command will work dependably only with Epson- or IBM PC-compatible printers, which fortunately is the vast majority of the printers available today.

(4) Those using a printer designed to be hooked up to a computer using serial interface protocols will need to understand this use of **MODE**. Unless you specify otherwise otherwise, DOS will send data destined for a printer to the default printer port—usually LPT1. To send the data instead to a serial printer attached to COM2, for example, enter (or include in an AUTOEX-EC.BAT file): **MODE LPT1:=COM2.**

Printer redirection will usually be preceded by the serial port initialization procedure described under #2 above. To end redirection of printer output, enter: **MODE LPT1:.**

(5) More recent versions of DOS have an alternative and more explicit syntax for setting screen and printer parameters. To set up for 43 lines by 80 columns onscreen, assuming your hardware can handle that format, type:

MODE CON COLS=80 LINES=43

To set up the printer for eight lines per inch and 132 columns per line, type:

MODE LPT1 COLS=132 LINES=8

Acceptable values for columns are 80 and 132, and for lines, 6 and 8.

(6) Most PC keyboards have a "typematic" function whereby any key that is held down for a certain length of time will be repeated onscreen. Recent DOS versions allow the user to vary the speed of repetition in characters sent to the screen per second, and modify the delay between the time the first character appears on the screen and the beginning of rapid repetition of characters. Experiment with the two parameters to see what suits you best.

(7) As use of code pages is rarely necessary, coverage of the topic is left to the documentation provided with DOS.

(8) As with specification of screen and printer formats, an effort has been made in recent DOS versions to provide a clearer means of setting the operating parameters of the communication port(s) attached to the PC.

Allowable Baud rates are 110, 150, 300, 600, 1200, 2400, 4800, 9600, and 19,200. PARITY can be ODD, EVEN, MARK, SPACE or NONE. DATA is the number of data bits to be used. STOP is the number of stop bits. RETRY specifies action to be taken if the port is busy.

Note: **MODE** commands are often included in an AUTOEXEC.BAT file in order to automatically set up one or more of the system's features for a particular function.

MODE can also be used in conjunction with Code Page Switching, a facility introduced with DOS 3.3 that allows for easier program support of multilingual character sets. As the topic seems more appropriate for programmers than for end-users, the interested reader is directed to DOS documentation and programming-oriented materials available from other published sources.

GRAPHICS
Screen Graphics on Printer

SYNTAX: (1) **GRAPHICS**
(2) **GRAPHICS** [printer] [/R I /B I /LCD] [profile]

PURPOSE: Allows the user to use Shift-PrtSc to print graphics images displayed onscreen, and supports printing on several specific printer models. (External)

SWITCHES: **/ R** Reverses black and white images
/ B With the COLOR4 and COLOR8 printers causes screen background color to be printed. It would not be printed otherwise.
/ L C D Prints content of a liquid crystal display

USAGE: Only the first syntax, compatible with the IBM Graphics Printer and compatibles, is supported through DOS 2.1. With DOS 3.0, 3.1, and 3.2 the IBM Color Printer (COLOR1 with a black ribbon; COLOR4 with a red, blue, and green ribbon; and COLOR8 with cyan, magenta, yellow, and black ribbon) is supported. DOS 3.3 adds support for the IBM Compact Printer (COMPACT) and the PC Convertible printer (THERMAL).

GRAPHICS is a terminate-and-stay-resident (TSR) program. It is run once, often from within a batch file, and it loads itself into memory for the rest of the user's session with the computer. Whenever output is directed to the printer with Shift-PrtSc, it goes into action, processing the screen image so that it will appear as desired on the printed page. To put GRAPHICS to work, type **GRAPHICS**.

The most recent versions of DOS support printer profile files. If the name of a file is given on the **GRAPHICS** command line, the profile it contains will be used in the printing of images from the screen. If no other file is indicated, the file GRAPHICS.PRO is used.

Hard Disk Management

Hard disk drives are making the transition from luxury to necessity. As software developers engage in Feature Wars, the size of the resulting packages grows apace. It is not unusual to receive the latest and greatest update of a major word-processing or database-management package on a dozen or so 360-KB floppy disks. While many packages can be installed for use on a dual-floppy computer system, the disk swapping necessary to get to the dictionary, thesaurus, or indexing routine is inconvenient and time-consuming.

With the cost of the devices spiraling ever downward, most libraries can easily afford the added convenience and increased speed of operation that come with a hard disk. Once you have your 20MB or 40MB of hard disk capacity, however, new problems can arise. Let's say you use an electronic spreadsheet, a word-processing program, a telecommunications program, and a database manager. The program files and files of associated material—printer drivers, parameter files, configuration files, tutorials, overlays, help files, etc.—can number in the hundreds.

When you can't remember the name of a program, typing **DIR** will fill eight or ten screens with a hodgepodge of filenames—not much help! As you copy programs from floppy to the hard disk drive, like filenames will overwrite one another. The READ.ME file associated with PC-File will be obliterated by the subsequently copied READ.ME from WordPerfect. The **DOS COPY** command will give no hint that this has happened. Now mix in some data files. After a few months, you could easily be awash among 500 or more disk files. Try hunting through that haystack 24 screen lines at a time!

DOS' answer to this potential mess is subdirectories. Instead of throwing all files into the same voluminous pot, users can create separate storage compartments, each designed to hold a specific type of file. They are free to create as many subdirectories as are needed, and to use whatever organizing principle they wish in determining which files go where. Subdirectories can be created within subdirectories, affording a high degree of hierarchy for those who wish to use it. While designed to meet the needs of hard disk users, subdirectory commands work equally well on floppy disks.

The new DOS Shell introduced with version 4.0 of DOS has its greatest utility in working with the large numbers of files and subdirectories typical of a hard disk drive. If you are using version 4.0 or higher, you may wish to glance quickly over the following material and then jump directly to the DOS Shell chapter. Most of what is described here can be done more quickly and easily from within the Shell.

The top-level directory on any disk is called the root directory. It is indicated by the backslash, " \ ." CONFIG.SYS and AUTOEXEC.BAT have to be in the root directory, but just about every other file on a disk can be consigned to its own subdirectory. The FORMAT.EXE program is stored in the DOS subdirectory. It can be invoked by:

C:\>   C:\DOS\FORMAT   A:

MKDIR, CHDIR, and **RMDIR** are used to manage creation, use, and removal of subdirectories. **PATH** is an extremely important command for hard disk users as it allows for convenient use of programs irrespective of which directory they are stored in. **TREE** displays a list of the subdirectory structure in place on a disk. **BACKUP** and **RESTORE** are often used to make secure copies of the programs and data residing on the hard drive. **FDISK** is a disk-partitioning routine that users should know about if they will ever have to reformat a hard disk.

MKDIR/MD
Makes Directory

SYNTAX: **MD** [drive] <subdirectory name>
    MKDIR [drive] <subdirectory name>

PURPOSE: Creates a new subdirectory. (Internal)

USAGE: To create a tutorial directory within the C:\DBASE subdirectory, you could enter: **MD C:\DBASE\TUTORIAL.**

RMDIR/RD
Removes Directory

SYNTAX: **RD** [drive] <subdirectory name>
    RMDIR [drive] <subdirectory name>

PURPOSE: Removes a previously created subdirectory. (Internal)

USAGE: Only an empty subdirectory can be removed. An error message will be displayed if you try to remove a subdirectory with files in it. Use **DEL** or **ERASE** to get rid of files first. Some program installation processes create hidden and read-only files, the names of which will not be displayed by the **DIR** command. To delete a hidden file in a subdirectory use one of the utilities described in the "Supplementing DOS" chapter. My favorite is the Still River Shell. It displays hidden files and allows you to change them to visible, or to just delete them irrespective of their status. To remove the tutorial directory created previously, enter:

RD   C:\DBASE\TUTORIAL

> **CHDIR/CD**
> **Changes Directory**

SYNTAX: CHDIR [drive] <subdirectory name>

PURPOSE: Designates a new subdirectory as the default subdirectory. (Internal)

USAGE: Subdirectories behave in many respects like disk drives. Just as there is a default disk drive at all times, there is a default subdirectory as well. The root directory is the default subdirectory until the user logs onto some other subdirectory.

In order to run a program, you must (1) be logged onto the subdirectory in which it is stored; (2) specify the full pathname of the directory in which it is stored as part of the file specification for the program; or (3) have used the **PATH** command to specify certain subdirectories that are to be searched when a program is not in the current or designated subdirectory (see **PATH**).

To change to the tutorial subdirectory within the dBase subdirectory, you enter:

C:\>   CD C:\DBASE\TUTORIAL
C:\DBASE\TUTORIAL>

To return to the root directory from anywhere within the subdirectory structure, enter:

```
C:\DBASE\TUTORIAL>  CD \
C:\
```

Here's a handy shortcut for navigating among disk directories. To jump up one level in the subdirectory hierarchy, use ".." the "double dot":

```
C:\DBASE\TUTORIAL>   CD ..
C:\DBASE>
```

PATH
Sets Search Path for Locating Program Files

SYNTAX: PATH [[drive:]subdirectory;[drive:]subdirectory;etc.]

PURPOSE: Provides DOS with a list of subdirectories to be searched for an executable program whenever that program is not present in the default or otherwise designated subdirectory. (Internal)

USAGE: Here's a typical **PATH** command line from the AUTOEXEC.BAT file of my computer:

PATH   c:\util;c:\bin;c:\dos;c:\;c:\ws5;c:\dbase;c:\dbxl

As I work in the C:\BOOK directory, I can invoke WordStar Release 5 simply by typing **WS**. DOS looks for WS in the \BOOK directory first, then in \UTIL, \BIN, \DOS, the root directory indicated by the backslash alone, then \WS5. The search will stop there because there is an executable file named WS present in WS5. To get the fastest response, place the subdirectories of the most used programs first in the **PATH** list. Be sure that every subdirectory in the list exists. If a subdirectory doesn't exist, DOS will stop scanning at that point and subsequently named subdirectories will be ignored. Be sure as well that there are no spaces between subdirectory names and semicolons. A single space will invalidate all subdirectory names appearing after it.

PATH helps DOS find executable programs, e.g., files ending in .EXE, .COM, or .BAT. It will not assist DOS in locating data files. Use the **APPEND** command for locating data files.

PATH alone displays the path currently in effect. There is a limit of 128 characters on the total path specification.

APPEND
Sets Search Path for Locating Data Files

SYNTAX: APPEND <[drive:]subdirectory;[drive:]subdirectory;etc.>   [/X |
/E]

PURPOSE: Provides DOS with a list of subdirectories to be searched for
any file, executable or not, that is not present in the current default subdirectory. (Internal)

SWITCHES: /X Instructs DOS to follow the path specified in the **AP-**
PEND list when searching for files that a program or
DOS command is to act upon (e.g., COPY, REN, etc.).
 /E Stores the **APPEND** string in the DOS environment so
that it can be (1) more easily accessed by programs designed to look to the environment and (2) more readily
changed by such programs.

USAGE: APPEND is similar in function to the **PATH** command. It locates data files while **PATH** locates executable (i.e., program) files. To specify a list of subdirectories to be searched, enter:

APPEND   C:\LETTERS;C:\;C:\MEMOS

If you need to **TYPE, COPY,** or **DEL** a file located in any one of
several possible subdirectories, **APPEND** with the /X parameter may be of
some help. The /X parameter must be present at the first issuance of the **AP-**
PEND command in order for DOS to use it to track down files required by
DOS commands. Unfortunately, **APPEND** used in this way can also make
it easier to mistake files with like names for one another and delete, rename,
or otherwise change them in ways you might not wish to.

Be particularly careful when using **APPEND** with any program that
makes changes to a data file once it is located. The newest version of the data
file will be saved in the current subdirectory, not in the subdirectory where the
original was found. You could easily end up with multiple, updated versions
of a file containing nearly the same information and no easy way to merge
them.

The length of the path list is limited to 128 characters. To view the current path, just type **PATH:**

PATH

PATH=C:\UTIL;C:\BIN;C:\DOS;C:\;C:\WS5;C:\DBASE;
C:\DBXL

```
┌─────────────────────────┐
│          TREE           │
│    Lists  Subdirectories │
└─────────────────────────┘
```

SYNTAX: TREE [drive:] [/F I /A]

PURPOSE: Displays a list of the subdirectories of a drive and, optionally, the files in each. (External)

SWITCHES: / F List files as well as the subdirectories in which they reside.

/ A Use alternate set of graphics characters (+, -, I, and \) that are universal across code pages.

USAGE: TREE offers a primitive means of viewing the full directory structure of a disk drive. The file manager provided with DOS 4.0 or a utility program like Still River Shell or Xtree gives a much better view of what is where, along with the tools to manipulate files and subdirectories. To view subdirectories, type:

TREE C:

The first few lines of the response on my system are:

DIRECTORY PATH LISTING

Path: C:\DEV
Sub-directories: None

Path: C:\DOS
Sub-directories: None

Path: C:\UTIL
Sub-directories: None

Path: C:\KIDS
Sub-directories: None

Path: C:\COPTER
Sub-directories: None

Path: C:\GENIFER
Sub-directories: BIBDIR
                TEST

Path: C:\GENIFER\BIBDIR
Sub-directories: None

Path: C:\GENIFER\TEST
Sub-directories: None

You'll need to be quick with the Ctrl-S to pause the display. Otherwise, the listing will whiz by and you will likely miss what you are looking for.

The /F switch produces a list of all files on the disk, organized by sub-directory. It may be useful in isolated circumstances. Combining it with the output redirection operator ">," you can create a disk file containing all the filenames and paths of every file on a disk:

TREE C: /F > FILELIST.TXT

Here's a segment of the list produced:

DIRECTORY PATH LISTING

Path: C:\DEV

Sub-directories: None

Files: HITACHI   .SYS

Path: C:\DBXL

Sub-directories: UTILS
                  TOOLS

Files: DBXL   .EXE
                DBXL   .MSG
                DBXL   .OV1

```
CONFIG      .XL
BUILDWIN    .EXE
MODISCN     .EXE
MODISCN     .HLP
DBXL        .HLP
DBXL        .OV2
INSTALL     .EXE
INSTALL     .DAT
INSTALL     .TXT
SETUP       .EXE
DBCON       .EXE
CONFIG      .DB3
CHECKCOM.BIN
GETCOM      .BIN
READ        .ME
FLOW        .EXE
ARC         .EXE
DB3SGEN     .COM
DB3SGEN     .DOC
DB3SGEN     .HLP
TEST        .SCN
TEST        .PRG
```

Path: C:\DBXL\UTILS

Sub-directories: None

Files:
```
READ ME     .UTL
SAYWHATL .BIN
SWITCHAR .COM
FLASHCDE .PRG
SAYWHATL .ASM
SAYWHAT1 .PRG
VIDPOP      .PRG
DFIXUP      .TXT
DFIXUP      .PRN
DFIXUP      .EXE
```

Path: C:\DBXL\TOOLS

Sub-directories: None

Files: WRAPPER .PRG
                      TEST   .DBF
                      MENUSKEL .PRG
                      SPECMENU .DBF
                      SPECORDR .NDX

See **TREED** in the "Supplementing DOS" chapter for a public-domain alternative that improves upon **TREE**.

BACKUP
Makes Backup Copies of Files

SYNTAX: BACKUP <filespec> <drive:> [/S | /M | /A | /L | /T | /D]

PURPOSE: Makes a backup copy on disk of one or more files from your hard disk drive. (External)

SWITCHES: / S   Include in the backup all subdirectories below the designated directory.

   / M   Back up only the files changed since the last backup.

   / A   Add the files being backed up to files that were already present on the floppy disk, rather than overwriting them.

   / L   Create a log file called BACKUP.LOG that contains the date, time, filename, and disk number of the backup, and place it in the root directory of the hard drive.

   / T   Back up those files created on or after the designated time.

   / D   Back up those files created on or after the designated date.

USAGE: BACKUP copies hard disk files on one or as many disks as necessary. (Actually, it will copy floppy disk files as well, though this makes little sense unless you are backing up a higher capacity disk onto a drive with lower capacity.) Unlike **COPY** or **XCOPY**, **BACKUP** stores copied files in an unreadable form. You cannot use files created by **BACKUP** until they are **RESTORE**d again to a disk large enough to accommodate them. Also unlike **COPY** and **XCOPY**, **BACKUP** can split a file across multiple floppy disks.

BACKUP automatically formats a disk if it has not already been formatted. Each disk is given a number which you should write on its external label. BACKUP turns off the "archive bit" associated with every file that is backed up. DOS will automatically turn the archive bit back on if changes are made to the file, making it eligible for backing up again. The ATTRIB command can be used to turn the archive on or off independent of BACKUP. To back up all files and subdirectories on drive C:, type:

BACKUP C:*.*   A: /S

Here's the response when we back up the .DBF files in the \OD2 subdirectory:

BACKUP \OD2*.DBF   A:

Source disk is Non-removable

Insert backup disk 01 in drive A:

Warning! Files in the target drive
A:\ root directory will be erased
Strike any key when ready

*** Backing up files to drive A: ***
Disk Number: 01

\OD2\ITEMTEMP.DBF
\OD2\NADFIRST.DBF
\OD2\NADTEMP.DBF
\OD2\ITEMS.DBF
\OD2\BORROWER.DBF

Insert backup disk 02 in drive A:

Warning! Files in the target drive
A:\ root directory will be erased
Strike any key when ready

*** Backing up files to drive A: ***
Disk Number: 02

\OD2\BORROWER.DBF
\OD2\SCRSHELF.DBF
\OD2\NADBILL.DBF
\OD2\TEMPBORR.DBF
\OD2\TEMP.DBF
\OD2\SCRCALL.DBF
\OD2\SCRATCH.DBF

To back up only the contents of the \BOOK subdirectory, type:

BACKUP C:\BOOK   A:

Individual files can be backed up as well. To add APPENDIX.DOS to the files already backed up on A:, type:

BACKUP C:\BOOK\APPENDIX.DOS   A: /A

To back up just the files that have changed since the last backup, those with their archive bit set on, enter:

BACKUP C: A: /M

The /T and /D switches allow you to back up based on the time and date stamp applied to each file by DOS. The two switches can be used together or separately. Here, we back up everything in all subdirectories created after 3 P.M. on January 5, 1989:

BACKUP C:*.* A: /S /T:15:00 /D:01–05–89

Finally, a log file can be created with the following command line:

BACKUP C:*.*   A: /L

```
                        RESTORE
          Copies  Backup  Files  Back  to  Hard  Disk
```

SYNTAX: RESTORE <drive:> <filespec>

PURPOSE: Copies to a drive the files backed up during a previous use of the **BACKUP** command. (External)

SWITCHES: /S   Restore all files in subdirectories.

/M   Restore only the files changed since the last backup.

/N   Restore only those files that no longer exist on the target drive (normally drive C:).

/P   DOS will prompt the user as to whether or not a read-only file or a file changed since the last time it was backed up should be replaced by an older backup file.

/B   Restore only those files created on or before the designated date.

/A   Restore only those files created on or after the designated date.

/L   Restore only those files created at or later than the designated time.

/E   Restore only those files created at or earlier than the designated time.

USAGE: RESTORE converts backup files that have been saved in a special archival format using the **BACKUP** command to files that once again can be used within DOS. *Be careful:* unless you include the /P switch, you can easily replace the most current version of a file with an older, non-current version that has been sitting in a disk box for a while.

To restore all files, including subdirectories, on the backup disks in drive A: to fixed disk drive C:, type:

RESTORE A: C:*.*   /S /N

To restore an individual file, type:

RESTORE A: C:\BOOK\NEXTBOOK

To restore .DBF files that were changed or deleted since they were last backed up, enter:

RESTORE A: C:*.DBF   /M

A variety of time and date specifications are possible (see the section on Switches, above). To restore only those file changed on or after January 5, 1988, type:

RESTORE A: C: /A:01–05–89

Filters, Redirection, and Pipes

A filter is a special kind of computer program that takes the output of some other program, manipulates it, and passes it on, often to another program. What comes out is different from what went in.

The collection of little stand-alone programs you get with DOS—the manual refers to them as "external commands"—includes at least the FIND, SORT, and MORE filters discussed later. They are like sections of model railroad track in that they can be strung together to create a surprisingly sophisticated processing layout.

In the "real world," relatively few computer users make use of the DOS filters. This may be because applications programs perform the same functions better. It also may be due to the relatively small amount of time most computer users have to master what is, after all, far from the most important of DOS commands. Users, rightly, focus on getting the most from their applications programs and learn only the DOS facilities that they need to know to make the applications work. Inclusion of filters in this section reflects their potential usefulness in special circumstances.

By its nature, a filter processes data on its way from one place to another. The "<" operator indicates that a filter should take its input from a particular file or device (the console, the communications port). The ">" operator instructs DOS to transfer the output of a filter to a named file or device (printer or communications port).

It is possible to automatically feed the results of one program directly to another without storing intermediate results in a disk file (if all programs use "standard input" and produce "standard output"). Most DOS commands and small utility programs do just that; most large applications programs do not. The process by which the output of one command becomes the input of another is called "piping." The "|" character indicates that the results of executing various programs are to be piped from program to program as indicated by a left-to-right reading of a command line.

To produce a directory of files created on a specific day in order by time of creation, you could use piping, creating the following listing:

DIR | FIND "9-18-88" | SORT /+34

JUNK4   **2052**   **9-18-88**   **3:35p**

JUNK	BAT	110	9-18-88	4:49p
BATCH	DOS	11392	9-18-88	5:05p
TREE	FI	4096	9-18-88	5:43p
TREELIST		56647	9-18-88	5:45p
ADDL	BAK	2176	9-18-88	12:04a
TIPS	DOS	9088	9-18-88	12:09a

If you need to put together such specialized command sequences as the one above, consider the filters and associated redirection and piping operators as an erector set with which to construct your own DOS utility programs. Keep in mind as well that there may be a public-domain utility program that does the job faster while demanding less of the user. Finding just what you need is the hard part there.

FIND
Finds a String of Characters in a File

SYNTAX: FIND [/V][/C][/N] <"text to find"> <filespec> [filespec] [file-spec]...

PURPOSE: Locates a specified text string in a file or files and, optionally, displays the lines in which it appears with or without line numbers, or a count of the number of lines in which it appears. (External)

SWITCHES: / V Display the lines that don't have the specified text.
/ C Report a count of the number of lines with the string. Don't display strings.
/ N Display line numbers indicating the relative position of each line within its file.

USAGE: FIND is likely to be of greatest use when a quick, no-fuss means of searching a file for a given word or phrase is called for. Perhaps you can't remember which file contains the fund-raising letter for Widget Corporation. **FIND** "Widget Corp" may be a quick way of locating what you want. While **FIND** has the potential for use in a make-shift, database-searching role, an applications program designed for that purpose is far more versatile

We will work with a simple text file called TEST.FIL. It contains abbreviated author and title listings exported from a dBase-compatible database file. We can find the contents of the file by typing it:

TYPE TEST.FIL

Rush, Robert	From conception to birth;
Flanagan, Geraldi	The first nine months of life.
Rodale	Practical Homeowner
	The Nature Conservancy News Jun
Pollock, Bruce	When the music mattered
Canby	Study of the short story
	The book of the horse
Findley & Findley	Your rugged Constitution
Lindbergh	North to the Orient
Woolf ed.	Writer's Diary
Woolf	Moments of being
Lennon	Victorica through the looking g
Boxer	Chemistry subject test
Berezin	The gentle birth book

To locate the books with "birth" in the title, enter:

```
FIND "birth" TEST.FIL
——————— TEST.FIL
```

| Rush, Robert | From conception to birth; |
| Berezin | The gentle birth book |

Let's produce a list of author-title lines *without* the word "birth":

```
FIND /V "birth" TEST.FIL

——————— TEST.FIL
```

Flanagan, Geraldi	The first nine months of life.
Rodale	Practical Homeowner
	The Nature Conservancy News Jun
Pollock, Bruce	When the music mattered
Canby	Study of the short story
	The book of the horse
Findley & Findley	Your rugged Constitution
Lindbergh	North to the Orient
Woolf ed.	Writer's Diary
Woolf	Moments of being
Lennon	Victorica through the looking g
Boxer	Chemistry subject test

Finally, we'll just count the number of lines in which "birth" appears:

FIND /C "birth" TEST.FIL

— — — — — TEST.FIL: 2

FIND will not accept wildcards, unfortunately. It will process a series of file specifications entered in series as part of the **FIND** command line. To look for "birth" in TEST.FIL, BIB.TXT, and BK.LST, type:

FIND "birth"   TEST.FIL   BIB.TXT   BK.LST

| **SORT** |
| Sorts Line by Line |

SYNTAX: SORT [/R][/+start position] < <source device or file>

PURPOSE: Sorts incoming data line by line. (External)

SWITCHES: / R   Sort in reverse order.
/ + n   Sort starting at character position designated by "n."

USAGE: We will use the short data file introduced in the discussion of the **FIND** command to demonstrate use of **SORT**. To sort the file by author (character-by-character from position 1 onwards), enter:

SORT < TEST.FIL

	The Nature Conservancy News Jun
	The book of the horse
Berezin	The gentle birth book
Boxer	Chemistry subject test
Canby	Study of the short story
Findley & Findley	Your rugged Constitution
Flanagan, Geraldi	The first nine months of life.
Lennon	Victorica through the looking g
Lindbergh	North to the Orient
Pollock, Bruce	When the music mattered
Rodale	Practical Homeowner
Rush, Robert	From conception to birth;
Woolf	Moments of being
Woolf ed.	Writer's Diary

To sort the lines in reverse order and store the result in a disk file called TEST.REV, type:

SORT /R < TEST.FIL   > TEST.REV

Note that action takes place from left to right. First the sort is done and only then does anything get redirected to the TEST.REV file. That file looks like this:

TYPE TEST.REV

Woolf ed.	Writer's Diary
Woolf	Moments of being
Rush, Robert	From conception to birth;
Rodale	Practical Homeowner
Pollock, Bruce	When the music mattered
Lindbergh	North to the Orient
Lennon	Victorica through the looking g
Flanagan, Geraldi	The first nine months of life.
Findley & Findley	Your rugged Constitution
Canby	Study of the short story
Boxer	Chemistry subject test
Berezin	The gentle birth book
	The book of the horse
	The Nature Conservancy News Ju

Here, we will find lines that contain "The," then sort them on the basis of character 24 and beyond, effectively alphabetizing by the first word after the "The" at the beginning of the title. Notice the use of the piping operator "|" which causes the output of the **FIND** program to become the input of the **SORT** program:

FIND "The" < TEST.FIL | SORT /+24

	The Nature Conservancy News Jun
	The book of the horse
Flanagan, Geraldi	The first nine months of life.
Berezin	The gentle birth book

```
                    MORE
    Pauses for Each Screen of Information
```

SYNTAX: MORE < \<source device or file\>

PURPOSE: Displays information from the designated source one screen at a time. After every 23 lines, scrolling pauses and "—More—" is displayed at the bottom left of the screen. (External)

USAGE: To cause the display of a file called BIG.LST to pause each time the screen fills, type: **MORE < BIG.LST.** "—More—" will be displayed after the first screen fills. Pressing any key will bring a second group of 23 lines to the screen followed by another "—More—."

You can pipe the output of a program or DOS command that creates standard screen output to the MORE filter in order to more easily view that output. **TREE** is a good example of a command that benefits from having its output piped through the MORE filter:

TREE | MORE

DIRECTORY PATH LISTING FOR VOLUME OLD-FAITHFUL

Path: C:\DEV

Sub-directories: None

Path: C:\DOS

Sub-directories: None

Path: C:\UTIL

Sub-directories: None

Path: C:\KIDS

Sub-directories: None
— More —

Miscellaneous

JOIN
Joins Files from Multiple Drives

SYNTAX: JOIN <drive> [drive:directory I /D]

PURPOSE: Logically connects a subdirectory on one drive with the files on another disk drive. (External)

SWITCHES: / D Remove current join with respect to named physical drive.

USAGE: The subdirectory to which the contents of a physical disk are assigned must be empty. If it doesn't exist when named in the **JOIN** command, it will automatically be created.

The contents of B: will appear to be held in C:\TEMP if the following command line is executed: **JOIN B: C:\TEMP**.

The current **JOIN** relationship can be displayed by typing **JOIN**:

JOIN
B: => B;C:\TEMP

To terminate the **JOIN** relationship, type:

JOIN A: /D

SUBST
Substitutes a Drive Letter for a Pathname

SYNTAX: SUBST [drive:] [[drive:]path list]

PURPOSE: Assigns a dummy drive designation to a subdirectory as a means of making the use of extended pathnames more convenient. (External)

USAGE: You have 30MB of files spinning around your hard drive. Nearly 2,000 individual filenames are stuck in their cubby holes (read subdirectories). And there are *many* subdirectories! Perhaps you have to type a file specification like this to edit a letter:

WS   C:\PROJECT5\SECTION3\LETTERS\SMITHCO.LTR

Ugh. There has to be a better way. **SUBST** offers one alternative. We'll refer to the long pathname as D:. Here's the substitution followed by the new command line for getting into the document SMITHCO.LTR:

SUBST D: C:\PROJECT5\SECTION3\LETTERS
WS D:SMITHCO.LTR

You can use any drive letter as long as it isn't greater than the letter designated by **LASTDRIVE** in the CONFIG.SYS file. **SUBST** can be used to create multiple drive definitions.

To end the substitution, type:

SUBST D: /D

Each substitution must be deactivated individually.

Typing **SUBST** alone displays the substitutions currently in effect:

D: => C:\PROJECT5\SECTION3\LETTERS

Back a few years ago, WordStar and a number of less-popular programs were too antiquated to allow for pathnames as part of a file specification. **SUBST** allowed the user to make a subdirectory look just like a separate drive from the viewpoint of the applications program.

Confusion can result if any of the following commands are used when **SUBST** is in effect:

- **FORMAT**
- **JOIN**
- **DISKCOPY**
- **DISKCOMP**
- **ASSIGN**
- **BACKUP**
- **RESTORE**
- **VOL**
- **LABEL**

ASSIGN
Assigns One Drive to Another

SYNTAX: ASSIGN <drive to be redirected>=<drive to receive data>

PURPOSE: Causes programs that normally work with a particular drive to automatically work with another designated drive. (External)

USAGE: ASSIGN allows one disk drive to masquerade as another. If you work with a program that insists on saving data on drive B:, and you would rather it worked with drive C:, just enter: **ASSIGN B=C**. All subsequent activity involving B will be channeled to C instead. Note that it is not necessary to include colons in the drive designations.

More than one assignment can be issued. To direct calls for A: and C: to B:, type: **ASSIGN A=B   C=B**. To end all current assignments, just type: **ASSIGN**.

ASSIGN can be extremely dangerous. If you or a co-worker forgets, for instance, that B: is assigned to C:, a command to **FORMAT B:** could clobber your hard drive instead. It is easy to get confused doing deletions and other common housekeeping operations when **ASSIGN** is in effect. Check whether **JOIN** or **SUBST** can help you more safely achieve your objectives.

RECOVER
Recovers Parts of Damaged Files

SYNTAX: RECOVER <filespec | drive:>

PURPOSE: Recovers as much as possible of a damaged disk file or of an entire disk that has sustained damage. (External)

USAGE: To recover whatever is readable in DAMAGED.FIL, enter:

RECOVER DAMAGED.FIL

If DAMAGED.FIL is a text file, the readable portion of it will be recovered and placed in a new file called DAMAGED.FIL where it can be examined and used again. If a program file has been damaged, chances are good that the recovered portion will be of no use.

You can **RECOVER** either one file at a time or the disk as a whole. If you wish to **RECOVER** an entire disk at once, **RECOVER** will step through it, recovering each file whether it is damaged or not. Recovered files are stored as FILE0001.REC, FILE0002.REC, etc. To initiate recovery of drive C:, the command is **RECOVER C:**.

VOL
Reports Volume Label

SYNTAX: VOL [drive:]

PURPOSE: Displays the volume label of the drive designated (the default drive if none is specified). (Internal)

USAGE: You can attach an internal label to a floppy or hard disk using **LABEL** or **FORMAT /V. VOL** allows you to view that label:

VOL B:
Volume in drive B is BEISERDISK

LABEL
Gives Volume Label to Drive

SYNTAX: LABEL [drive:] [volume label]

PURPOSE: Creates, changes an internal label on a hard or floppy disk. (External)

USAGE: LABEL was new with DOS 3.0. Prior versions didn't allow users to modify a label once it had been created or to add a label after the **FORMAT** operations had been completed. The only way to add a label was through the **FORMAT /V** command.

Volume labels can be up to 11 characters long. A typical session with **LABEL**:

LABEL

Volume in drive C has no label
Volume label (11 characters, ENTER for none)?
        OLDFAITHFUL

From now on, **DIR** and any other command that looks at the volume label of drive C: will find OLDFAITHFUL.

PRINT
Sends One or More Files to the Printer

SYNTAX: PRINT <filename(s)> [/D | /C | /T | /Q | /P | /B | /M | /U | /S]

PURPOSE: Prints or cancels printing of one or more files. (External)

SWITCHES: / D   Specify a print device other than the current default print device, allowing the user to alternate between several printer ports.

/ C   Cancel the printing of a named file held in the print queue.

/ T   Cancel the printing of all files in the queue.

/ Q   Adjust the number of files that can be held in the print queue from the default of 4. Maximum is 32.

/ P   Indicate that the filename to which it is attached, and all subsequent filenames, are to be added to the print queue, notwithstanding a preceding /C cancel instruction. If there is no /C to counteract, /P is not needed.

/ B   Adjust the size of the internal memory buffer between 512 and 16,000 bytes.

/ M   Determine how many "clock ticks" (i.e., what proportion of the microprocessor's attention) **PRINT** can have in which to send information to the printer. The range is from 1 to 255, with 2 the default.

/ U   Determine the number of clock ticks **PRINT** will wait for the printer to be ready. The range is 1 to 255 and the default is 1.

/ S   Determine the "time slice value," with a range of 1 to 255 and a default of 10.

USAGE: There are many ways to cause information stored in electronic form to be printed. Just about every applications program includes printing routines. In the case of word processors, those print routines are very sophisticated.

From the DOS prompt, you can send a text file (one without unprintable control characters) to the printer with:

COPY   myfile.txt   PRN:

The Shift-PrtSc key combination will print a screen full of information. Ctrl-PrtSc will echo everything sent to the screen to the printer. You can also use the DOS redirection operators:

TYPE   myfile.txt   >   PRN:

PRINT offers a method of producing printed output considerably more sophisticated than any of these other DOS possibilities. With it you can initiate the printing of a series of files, designated by filename or included in a wildcard specification:

PRINT   file1.txt   file2.txt   *.prg

The first file begins printing immediately. Other files are lined up in a print queue, awaiting their turn. While this is going on, the user can move on to using another computer program. **PRINT** will continue to parcel out information to the printer in the background.

The /B, /M, /U, and /S switches control the amount of memory and the proportion of microprocessor attention devoted to the background print task. The optimum settings will differ from computer system to computer system. If the defaults don't satisfy you in term of response time or printer speed, try changing the values of these switches one at a time. The general form is:

PRINT *.prg   /B:16000   /M:5   /U:1   /S:3

To cancel the printing of a file in the print queue called MYFILE.TXT, enter **PRINT   myfile.txt   /C.**

The peculiar /P switch is only required when you choose to both add to and delete from the print queue in one command line:

PRINT   myfile.txt   /C   myother.txt   /P   *.DOC

If it were not for the /P, the files MYFILE.TXT and MYOTHER.TXT, and the *.DOC files, would all be removed from the print queue.

PRINT is terrific for more technical users who work with extensive files of program source code that are in plain text format. It is also handy if you work with the online documentation that comes with many programs, particularly those that are distributed as shareware. Most average users will employ the printing facilities of a word-processing program rather than working with **PRINT**.

VERIFY
Verifies That Copy Operations Are Successful

SYNTAX: VERIFY [ON I OFF]

PURPOSE: Switches on and off the practice of reading all copied files to verify that they have been copied without error. (Internal)

USAGE: VERIFY alone indicates the current **VERIFY** state—on or off. **COPY** with the /V switch causes the same checks to be performed for a given copying operation as does **VERIFY**.

SYS
Puts System Files on Disk

SYNTAX: SYS <drive:>

PURPOSE: Transfers the hidden operating system files to a disk. (External)

USAGE: SYS can be used to install on a blank, formatted disk the two hidden files that must be on any bootable system disk. It can also be used to install a new version of DOS on a disk that was originally formatted with the **FORMAT** /S command. The **FORMAT** /B command formats a disk in such a way that space is allocated for the hidden system files even though they are not transferred at the time of formatting. **SYS** will install the system files on this type of disk as well. **SYS** will not install system files on a disk formatted without the /S or /B options if that disk already has data files recorded on it.

VER
Displays Version Info

SYNTAX: VER

PURPOSE: Displays the version number of the currently running version of DOS. (Internal)

USAGE: Use of the command results in the following dialogue:

```
C> VER
MS-DOS Version 3.21
C>
```

```
ATTRIB
Changes File Attributes
```

SYNTAX: ATTRIB [+R | -R | +A | -A] <filespec> [/S]

PURPOSE: Modifies the file attributes assigned to disk files. (External)

SWITCHES: +R Turn the read-only attribute on, making it impossible to delete or overwrite the file.
- **-R** Remove the read-only attribute.
- **+A** Turn on the archive bit of a file, indicating that it has not been backed up.
- **-A** Turn off the archive bit, preventing its being copied by the **BACKUP** command.
- **/S** Process all the files in the specified directory and in any subdirectories below it.

USAGE: The read-only attribute is a first line of defense against accidental deletion of important files on your hard disk drive. Far more people know how to delete with the **DEL** command than know how to override read-only protection with the **ATTRIB** command. If you are serious about using such protection, perhaps in an environment where several people uneasily share a hard drive, you might remove ATTRIB.EXE from the hard drive. Anyone wanting to make changes will then have to get a copy of it and use it from floppy disk.

To give MYTODO.LST read-only protection, I can enter **ATTRIB +R mytodo.lst**.

To turn the archive bit of all files on my hard drive on, preparatory to starting a new system of creating backup files using **BACKUP**, I could type **ATTRIB +A C:*.* /S**. The /S in combination with C:*.* causes all files in the root directory and all subdirectories under it to have their archive bits set on.

ATTRIB without an R or A switch reports the attributes of the file(s) referred to in the file specification. Here's a display of the archive attributes of the files in the \BOOK subdirectory:

```
C:\BOOK\>  ATTRIB *.*

A          C:\BOOK\APPENDIX.DOS
           C:\BOOK\DIR.SHT
A          C:\BOOK\SUPP.DOS
A          C:\BOOK\LIST.COM
A          C:\BOOK\NEXTBOOK
           C:\BOOK\TREE.FI
           C:\BOOK\MORE.SHT
```

Incidentally, DOS squawks "syntax error" if you try to inspect the archive bit status of files in multiple subdirectories using the /S switch.

Besides the read-only and archive attributes, files can also have hidden and system attributes. DOS provides no mechanism for changing these, but some of the utilities discussed in the "Supplementing DOS" chapter do.

DISKCOPY
Makes a Duplicate of a Disk

SYNTAX: DISKCOPY [drive:] [drive:]

PURPOSE: Makes an exact copy of the contents of one floppy disk on another floppy disk. (External)

USAGE: A quick way to make a copy of a new piece of software is to enter **DISKCOPY A: B:**. Be sure you've got the drives in the correct order, source first and destination second, because **DISKCOPY** obliterates the existing contents of the destination disk.

If there are defects in the destination disk, **DISKCOPY** will ignore them, writing data over them. You may discover only much later that some portion of the data transferred with **DISKCOPY** is inaccessible.

DISKCOPY can only be used with two disk drives of the same format and capacity. As the standard PC configuration shifts from dual floppy systems to systems with a hard drive and a single floppy, **DISKCOPY** will be used less. That is just as well, as **COPY** and **XCOPY** are safer. If the target disk is not already formatted, **DISKCOPY** will format it.

Unlike **COPY** and **XCOPY**, **DISKCOPY** doesn't unfragment files as it copies them. The result could be less-than-optimum performance in terms of load time for program and data files. For more on file fragmentation, consult the "DOS Tips and Tricks" chapter.

FASTOPEN
Speeds Up the Loading of Files

SYNTAX: FASTOPEN <drive:>[=number of locations to store] [/X]

PURPOSE: Provides quick access to files and subdirectories recently used by the system. (External) (DOS 3.3)

SWITCHES: /X Use expanded memory to store the locations of recently used files and subdirectories. (DOS 4.0)

USAGE: Users frequently use the same file or subdirectory a number of times. **FASTOPEN** tells DOS to store in fast random-access memory some of the information it would otherwise have to look up every time prior to giving the user access to a given file. The number of locations to be stored has a range of 10 to 999, with a default value of 34. For every location stored, 35 bytes of RAM are lost to other programs.

To use **FASTOPEN** with drives C: and D:, type:

FASTOPEN   C:=50   D:=100.

REPLACE
Selectively Overwrites Files

SYNTAX: REPLACE <filespec> <drive:>[\path]

PURPOSE: Selectively replaces files on one drive and directory with those from another location.

SWITCHES: /A Copy to target disk only those files that match the file specification and are not already on the target disk and di-

rectory. Cannot use in combination with /U or /A.
/ P   Prompts the user to confirm each replacement.
/ R   Replaces files even if they are read-only.
/ S   Looks in all subdirectories of the target disk for files that match the file specification provided. Cannot use in combination with /A.
/ U   Replaces files on the target only if they are older than files with the same filename on the source disk. Cannot use in combination with /A.
/ W   Waits for user to insert a disk before replacing files.

USAGE: To replace all files on drive A: that end with .BK with matching filenames from C:\BOOK, type:

REPLACE C:\BOOK*.BK   A:

To replace all WordStar files on a hard drive with new files bearing the same filenames as the files they are to replace, in whatever directory the old files reside, enter:

REPLACE A:WS*.*   C:\   /S

REPLACE with the /U switch is a quick way to back up just new versions of files that have not previously been copied to a backup disk. It is more convenient than **XCOPY** or **BACKUP** with a date parameter.

5

ADDITIONAL DOS COMMANDS AND CONCEPTS

The commands and concepts discussed in the next few pages are of interest to a relatively small number of technically sophisticated users and users with unusual special requirements. They are listed here as a starting point for those few who may wish to seek out other sources to investigate the commands further.

The objective of this book is to call to your attention the commands and concepts that you will need most frequently in operating an IBM PC-compatible computer. Some of the facilities of DOS are not widely or frequently used. They are included for the benefit of programmers and advanced users, an audience different from that to which this presentation is directed. With each new version of DOS, there are more of these relatively esoteric commands added. Consult the DOS manual or programmer-oriented, third-party texts on those rare occasions when one of the following commands may be called for.

CHCP: Changes code page, making specific additional characters available for display or printing.

COMMAND: Invokes a "secondary command processor." Sometimes used in batch files under DOS 3.2 or earlier to make it possible to branch from within a batch file to another batch file and automatically return to the end of the second batch file.

COMP: Compares two files to see if they are exactly identical. Usually, file size, date, and time are enough to establish which of several files contains the information you seek.

COUNTRY: Specifies conventions for country-specific defaults for currency, capitalization, decimal separator, collating sequence, date, time, and folding format. Used with country codes and code pages listed in the DOS manual.

CTTY: Accepts input from and sends output to the serial port, rather than the keyboard and screen. Offers a raw approach to turning control of a computer over to someone connected by cable or modem from another computer.

Users with little expertise in the area will find file-transfer software a worthwhile alternative to cobbling together a link using **CTTY**.

DEBUG: A programmers utility for viewing and modifying program code. Contains mini-assembly language facility.

DISKCOMP: Compares two disks byte-by-byte and displays differences between them. Rarely needed.

EXE2BIN: Converts program files ending in .EXE to .COM program if they meet certain requirements. Primarily for programmers.

FCBS: Determines the number of file control blocks that will be used in a networking situation. Usually taken care of automatically through network setup/installation routines.

FDISK: Creates and removes DOS partitions on hard disk drives preparatory to formatting. Renders data on drive inaccessible. Only necessary if you are working with a new hard disk that has never before been partitioned and formatted, or if you are changing a partition to accommodate DOS 4.0's new, larger maximum partition size.

GRAFTABL: Installs a user-specified set of screen-display characters. Used in conjunction with code-page switching in DOS 3.3 and higher.

KEYB: Loads a keyboard device driver specific to a particular national language keyboard offered by IBM. In DOS 3.3 and higher, the keyboard designated must match with characters in the currently active code page.

LINK: Programming utility that finishes the job of converting original program code written in a higher-level language to an executable program module stored in machine language.

NLSFUNC: Specifies the name of a country-specific file of information indicating date, time, and currency formats.

SET: Places a string in the DOS environment for use by programs designed to look for such strings. If it is necessary to use **SET**, the publishers of an applications program will generally provide instructions on what to do with it.

SHARE: Supports file sharing and file locking. Used primarily by those designing networking system software. Network installation routines generally take care of issuing the appropriate **SHARE** commands.

SHELL: Tells DOS to load a command processor other than COM-MAND.COM. Can only be used from a batch file.

STACKS: Sets aside a specified number of stack frames to hold program interrupts.

SWITCHAR: Changes the character used to separate a DOS command from one of its available switch specifications from "/" to some other designated character.

6

BATCH FILES

Wouldn't it be wonderful if you didn't have to do so much typing to accomplish the housekeeping tasks that DOS allows you to perform? If you could store a series of commands and have them execute automatically any time you chose, the tedium and triviality of DOS syntax would be considerably lessened. The DOS Shell included with version 4.0 and higher is one answer. Another answer is the batch file.

DOS Batch files contain a series of commands of the exact same sort that may be issued from the DOS prompt. Applications programs and DOS commands may be run equally well from within a batch file. All batch files must end with the .BAT file extension. Without it DOS will not recognize them as batch files and the instructions they contain will not be executed.

Hmm...a collection of stored commands executed in sequence by a computer—that's our seat-of-the-pants definition of a "program!" Indeed, batch files are programs in their own right, albeit constructed within a highly restrictive syntax. Within the small repertoire of available batch file commands, several of the fundamental features of any programming language are present. You can use **IF** to branch among alternative sets of commands based on whether some condition is true or not. **FOR** offers a form of looping structure, especially in conjunction with **SHIFT**. **GOTO**, a programming construct infamous for the complex flow of control that can result from thoughtless use, offers an additional wild and woolly looping vehicle.

If "programming" makes you nervous, rest assured that batch file construction is a far cry from writing a world-class spreadsheet in C:. Call this activity "batch file construction," not "programming," if it makes you more comfortable. If you aren't put off, however, consider yourself a programmer/ entry-level after you create your first batch file. You deserve a **BREAK** today!

Creating Batch Files

A batch file can be created using the **COPY CON** approach, a word processor capable of creating a pure text file (no weird embedded control characters), or a stand-alone editor such as the **EDLIN** editor included with DOS.

To illustrate the first method, we will use **COPY CON** to create STAR.BAT, a batch file that runs WordStar, deletes the backup files that it automatically creates, and copies files ending in .TXT to the floppy disk in drive A:

```
COPY CON STAR.BAT
ECHO OFF
CLS
WS
DEL *.BAK
ECHO Put the backup disk for w/p files in drive A:
COPY C:*.TXT A:
PAUSE ^Z
```

The "^Z" is read as "Ctrl-Z." It can be inserted by pressing F6 or by holding down the Ctrl key and pressing Z.

COPY CON has some limitations. You cannot edit an existing text file. You must retype the entire file to make even the smallest change and you can only work on the current line. The arrow keys will not allow you to move back up the screen again. If you spot an error on a line prior to the current one, you must do the whole thing over. **COPY CON** is a quick and dirty solution that works for short batch files. The longer the file you are creating, the less acceptable these limitations are.

Your favorite word-processing program may be a far superior alternative. It must, however, be capable of creating a text file that contains only seven-bit ASCII characters. The presence of the control characters often used internally to manage tabs, justification, centering, and such will cause your batch file to crash in flames. Many word processors have a "non-document" mode for creation of batch files. Others rely on the ability to "print to disk," that is, to create a disk file containing an exact image of what would have appeared if the file had been sent to the printer. Printing to disk has the effect of stripping off the unwanted control characters that DOS would choke on.

If you work with a dual floppy disk system, the large amount of disk space a word processor requires is a disadvantage. You will likely lose in swapping disks to get at the word processor much of what you have gained in abandoning the **COPY CON** method. If you have a hard drive, the only penalty you pay lies in the time required to load the word-processing program. For most of us, this is not a significant problem.

A text editor offers a compromise. It may offer the convenience of a word processor in a more compact, quicker-loading software package. Editors are designed solely to create disk files. Freed from the considerable overhead of functions that format text for printing, they can be "lean and mean." **EDLIN** comes with DOS. It is lean to the point of being emaciated, but may be entirely satisfactory for users who can become accustomed to its terse interface and exclusive line orientation.

A wide variety of full-screen editors are available that offer more features and are easier to learn. Check your source of shareware software for current revisions of full-screen editors.

Linking Batch Files

A batch file can be invoked from within another batch file by entering its name on a line by itself. Here, JOB1.BAT runs JOB2.BAT, which in turn runs JOB3.BAT. It is assumed that the batch files are all in a directory named in a **PATH** command.

```
TYPE JOB1.BAT
@ECHO OFF
DIR *.BK
PAUSE
CD \BOOK
JOB2

TYPE JOB2.BAT
@ECHO OFF
WS
ECHO Put floppy in drive A:
PAUSE
BACKUP C:\BOOK\*.BK A:
JOB3

TYPE JOB3
@ECHO OFF
ECHO Whew!! Glad that's over...
PAUSE
CD \
CLS
```

This is an example of "chaining" batch files together. Unfortunately, you can "jump" to a second batch file only once from within any given batch file.

The **CALL** command solves the problem. With it, you can branch to another batch file, then automatically return when it is finished running. You'll find more on **CALL** later in this chapter.

ECHO
Displays/Suppresses Display on Screen

SYNTAX: [@] **ECHO** <text string I OFF I ON>

PURPOSE: Displays a string of text on the computer screen from within a batch file and turns the echoing of command lines within a batch file off and on. (Internal)

USAGE: ECHO is most frequently used to take control of the onscreen display of command lines within a batch file. **ECHO OFF** suppresses display of any command lines that appear after it. Unfortunately, "**ECHO OFF**" is displayed on the screen before suppression takes place. Users of DOS 3.3 and higher can type **@ECHO OFF** to prevent the **ECHO** line from displaying. Those with high aesthetic standards and an earlier version of DOS can get the same effect by following **ECHO OFF** with a **CLS** (clear screen) command.

Once screen echo is off, **ECHO** can be used to send selected lines of text to the screen, instructing or informing the user. Here is a simple example of the use of **ECHO**:

```
ECHO  OFF
CLS
ECHO  Here's a directory of drive C:
DIR  C:*.DOS
```

The result of this batch file is:

```
Here's a directory of drive C:

Volume in drive C has no label
Directory of C:\BOOK

APPENDIX   DOS      384    9-10-88    11:01a
USEFUL     DOS    28032    9-17-88    10:48p
```

ESSEN	DOS	42240	9–17–88	10:26p
MASTER	DOS	256	9–10–88	11:00a
INDEX	DOS	256	9–10–88	11:01a
ADDL	DOS	2176	9–18–88	12:04a
GLOSS	DOS	18688	9–17–88	10:08p
INTRO	DOS	9344	9–17–88	10:48a
CONTENTS	DOS	3200	9–17–88	10:45a
TIPS	DOS	9088	9–18–88	12:09a
SUPP	DOS	29312	9–18–88	3:17p
BATCH	DOS	2560	9–18–88	3:33p

12 File(s)   3438592 bytes free

GOTO
Jumps Out of Sequence to Other Commands

SYNTAX: GOTO <:label name>

PURPOSE: Jumps from one part of a batch file to another, skipping some intervening command lines in the process. (Internal)

USAGE: A word preceded by a colon can serve as a label to which a batch file can jump with the GOTO instruction.

```
ECHO OFF
CLS
WS
DEL *.BAK
IF EXIST *.TXT GOTO :BACKUP
GOTO :FINISHED
:BACKUP
ECHO Put the backup disk for w/p files in drive A:
COPY C:*.TXT A:
PAUSE
:FINISHED
```

If there are any files that end in .TXT when the user exits WordStar (WS is its filename), the batch file jumps to the :BACKUP section to copy them to drive A:. If there are no such files, GOTO :BACKUP is ignored and GOTO :FINISHED is executed.

Beware of infinite loops. The following example will run until the computer is shut down or the user presses Ctrl-Break:

```
:BEGINNING
DIR B:
DIR A:
GOTO :BEGINNING
```

```
                          IF
            Branches on a Condition
```

SYNTAX: IF [NOT] <condition> <command>

PURPOSE: Performs a command if a given condition is true. Provides rudimentary branching facility for batch files. (Internal)

USAGE: IF provides a means for determining which of several possible actions will be taken. The batch file that follows illustrates how IF works. Called SAFEFORM.BAT, it puts a safety net under the FORMAT command, preventing the user from formatting the hard disk drive. It is assumed that FORMAT.EXE has been renamed ZZFORMAT. Without an .EXE or .COM file extension, you could run ZZFORMAT even if you wanted to.

```
@ECHO OFF
CLS
ECHO Safe Formatting
IF %1==C: GOTO :SORRY
IF %1==B: GOTO :NOB
:DOFORMAT
REN ZZFORMAT ZZFORMAT.EXE
ZZFORMAT %1
REN ZZFORMAT.EXE ZZFORMAT
GOTO :END
:SORRY
ECHO IT IS NOT A GOOD IDEA TO REFORMAT
YOUR ECHO HARD DISK DRIVE!!
GOTO :END
:NOB
ECHO There is no drive B: in this system.
ECHO If you wish, you can continue and DOS will
ECHO treat drive A: as alternately A: and B:
ECHO Press Ctrl-Break to stop right here.
PAUSE
GOTO :DOFORMAT
```

```
:END
PAUSE
CLS
```

To use SAFEFORM.BAT, type **SAFEFORM** <drive:>. **IF** controls which instructions are run, based on whether <drive:> is B:, C: or any other drive. If C: is the drive, the :SORRY routine says it will not operate on the hard disk and jumps to :END, at which point the batch file is finished. If B: is the drive, it offers the user the opportunity to break out of the batch file with Ctrl-Break instead of allowing DOS to use physical drive A: to serve as logical drive B:.

IF EXIST can be used to determine whether a particular file is present or not. Here is CHECKIT.BAT, a routine that checks for the presence of a READ.ME or README file and prints what it finds. It is invoked by typing **CHECKIT** <program name, no extension>. If a .DOC file exists and has a filename identical to the program name entered, it will be copied to drive C:.

```
IF EXIST A:READ.ME   PRINT A:READ.ME
IF EXIST A:README    PRINT A:README
IF EXIST A:%1.DOC   COPY A:%1.DOC   C:\DOCS\%1.DOC
```

IF NOT EXIST determines whether a given filename is absent and directs the actions of the batch file accordingly.

FOR
Works with a Group of Parameters

SYNTAX: FOR %%<variable> **IN** (<set>) **DO** <command>

PURPOSE: Causes a batch file to perform the same actions on each of a series of parameters, one at a time. (Internal)

USAGE: FOR can be used alone, at the system prompt, or within a batch file. If it is used within a batch file, the name of the dummy variable must be preceded by two percent signs rather than one.

The set may be a series of values or one value containing the * or ? wildcard characters. **FOR** will not proceed past a value containing a wildcard character.

Here, we use **FOR** to rename a group of files ending in .FOO. We will change their file extension to .BAK using the **FOR** command:

    C:\BOOK> FOR %A IN (*.FOO) DO REN %A *.BAK

    C:\BOOK> REN ADDL.FOO *.BAK
    C:\BOOK> REN GLOSS.FOO *.BAK
    C:\BOOK> REN BATCH.FOO *.BAK
    C:\BOOK> REN TEST.FOO *.BAK
    C:\BOOK> REN USEFUL.FOO *.BAK

If **FOR** is used within a batch file, the command would have to be changed to:

    C:\BOOK> FOR %%A IN (*.FOO) DO REN %%A *.BAK

Next, we delete the files JUNK, TEST.BAK, USEFUL.BAK, and BATCH.BAK by enumerating filenames within a FOR command:

    C:\BOOK> FOR %B IN (JUNK TEST.BAK USEFUL.BAK
                  BATCH.BAK) DO DEL %B

    C:\BOOK> DEL JUNK
    C:\BOOK> DEL TEST.BAK
    C:\BOOK> DEL USEFUL.BAK
    C:\BOOK> DEL BATCH.BAK

SHIFT
Works with More Than 10 Batch File Parameters

SYNTAX: SHIFT

PURPOSE: Makes it possible for a batch file to work with more than 10 parameters. (Internal)

USAGE: Replaceable parameters allow you to pass filename and other values to a batch file. Unfortunately, there is a maximum of 10 values, %0 through %9, that can be sent. **SHIFT** overcomes this restriction by shifting the definition of %0, %1, etc., one position to the left each time it is executed. The value in %2 becomes the value of %1, the value of %1 becomes the value assigned to %0, and the previous value of %0 disappears.

Here's a batch file called MULTIDEL.BAT that deletes files based on as many file specifications as you can fit on the command line:

```
:BEGINNING
IF NOT EXIST %1 GOTO :END
DEL %1
SHIFT
GOTO :BEGINNING
:END
```

One little trick is required to make this routine work. One or more characters that do not correspond to an existing filename must follow the last valid filename. If this is not done, the batch file will "hang" in a continuous loop after it has dealt with the last valid filename.

A typical command line for calling the batch file above might be:

MULTIDEL   *.BAK   *.BK   JUNK.BAT   TEMP1.*   x

PAUSE
Freezes Screen Display

SYNTAX: PAUSE [text]

PURPOSE: Causes the batch file to temporarily cease execution. (Internal)

USAGE: If you use **PAUSE** alone, the following will appear on the screen:

Strike any key when ready...

If you include a comment—21 characters maximum—and echoing of batch file commands to the screen has not been suppressed, then it will appear on the screen, followed by the "Strike any key..." instruction. Here's what "**PAUSE** Take a Deep Breath, then" will produce:

PAUSE Take a Deep Breath, then
Strike any key when ready...

This is messy at best. Rather than include a comment with **PAUSE**, turn **ECHO OFF** and use the **ECHO [text]** syntax to give instructions:

    @ECHO OFF
    ECHO Take a Deep Breath, then
    PAUSE

The result is:

    Take a Deep Breath, then
    Strike any key when ready...

REM
Remarks

SYNTAX: REM <text>

PURPOSE: Includes explanatory remarks in a batch file, both for the benefit of the creator of the batch file and for its users. (Internal)

USAGE: REM sends the designated text to the screen only when screen
echoing is on. The instruction **"REM What a day!!"** would appear as
REM What a day!!.

    Like **PAUSE, REM** is far from overwhelming as a means of inform-
ing the user of what is going on. Use **REM** to document your batch files so
you will know what is going on when you go back to make changes in the
future. **ECHO OFF** followed by **ECHO [text]** is the best way to commu-
nicate with the user.

BREAK
When to Check for Break

SYNTAX: BREAK <ON | OFF>

PURPOSE: Determines the frequency with which DOS checks to see
whether Ctrl-Break has been pressed to halt program execution. (Internal)

USAGE: To cause DOS to check more often for a Ctrl-Break, type
BREAK ON. To instruct DOS to check for Ctrl-Break less frequently, enter
BREAK OFF. BREAK alone reports the current **BREAK** status (on or
off).

CALL
Runs Another Batch File

SYNTAX: CALL <batch file name>

PURPOSE: Transfers control from one batch file to another in such a way that after the second batch file is finished, control returns to the first. (Internal)

USAGE: When a program that is a part of a batch file is exited, control returns to the batch file. This does not happen, however, when it is a batch file that is run from within a batch file. Let's say we have a batch file called MAIN.BAT and a second called WP.BAT. The XCOPY command in MAIN.BAT will never be executed because control goes back directly to DOS after WP.BAT is run.

```
TYPE MAIN.BAT

@ECHO OFF
DIR/W
PAUSE
WP.BAT
XCOPY C:\*.*  /S/M/W


TYPE WP.BAT

CLS
CD \WORK
WP
```

CALL was introduced to overcome this defect in the behavior of batch files. Making one change in MAIN.BAT ensures that the XCOPY command that backs up all changed files on the drives will be executed every time:

```
@ECHO OFF
DIR/W
PAUSE
CALL WP.BAT
XCOPY C:\*.*   /S/M/W
```

There is no limit to the number of times CALL can be used in a batch file. There is also no limit, other than available memory, to the degree of "nesting" (batch files calling batch files calling batch files).

Parameters may be passed on to a CALLed batch file. Let's say batch file NEWNAME.BAT contains the command **REN %1 %2**. When you initiate MAIN.BAT, the syntax is **MAIN** <filespec> <filespec>. MAIN.BAT uses the following instruction to bring NEWNAME.BAT into the action:

CALL NEWNAME %1 %2

A Batch File Menu System

Batch files can be used to create a simple menu system to make computer use simpler for those relatively unfamiliar with DOS commands and syntax. A file called MENU.BAT displays options. Files called 1.BAT, 2.BAT, 3.BAT, etc. actually execute the desired actions before reexecuting MENU.BAT to redisplay options.

TYPE MENU.BAT

ECHO OFF
CLS
ECHO Master Command Menu
ECHO <2 or more spaces>
ECHO 1. WordPerfect
ECHO 2. WordStar
ECHO 3. DBXL
ECHO 4. Check Disk
ECHO <2 or more spaces>
ECHO Enter your choice below

Here are two of the batch files called by MENU.BAT.:

TYPE 1.BAT

CHDIR \WRITING
WP
\MENU

TYPE 4.BAT

CHKDSK
\MENU

This approach will work for all versions of DOS.

Automatic Backup of Files

You should always back up any data files that are important to you. You probably should eat more vegetables and less fat as well. "Yes, but..." is the general response to such good advice.

Batch files can be used to make backing up data files a part of every session with the computer. If a reminder is all you need, you are one of the self-disciplined few. Your needs may be met by a batch file called WS.BAT.

```
@ECHO OFF
CLS
WSNEW
CLS
ECHO Be sure to back up any new or changed files!!
```

The WordStar word-processing program has been renamed WSNEW.EXE so that WS.BAT will be run when the user types **WS** at the prompt. After you exit from WordStar, the screen will clear and the message on the last line of the batch file will be displayed.

If this is too easy to ignore, then an approach that automatically copies files is called for. The **XCOPY** command is particularly useful as it copies from all subdirectories in one operation and looks at the archive attribute of each file.

```
@ECHO OFF
CLS
WSNEW
CLS
ECHO   New and changed files will be backed up now
XCOPY  C:\*.*  A:\  /W  /S  /M
```

The /W switch causes **XCOPY** to ask the user to insert a floppy disk before attempting to copy. The /S switch indicates that the contents of all subdirectories are to be scanned for files to be backed up. If you never edit files in more than one subdirectory while in WordStar (or whatever program you are using with this routine), and if you will be logged onto the subdirectory containing the text files that have been changed, then the command line could be reduced to **XCOPY *.* A:\ /W /M**.

The /M switch turns the archive bit off after each file is copied, ensuring that a given file will not be backed up a second time when WS.BAT is next invoked, unless it has been changed in the interim. The very first time, this batch file will attempt to back up every program and data file on the hard drive that has its archive bit set on. If this is not desirable, and if **BACKUP** or some other utility has not set the archive bit off already, you will have to go from subdirectory to subdirectory with the command **ATTRIB -A** **<\subdirectory*.*>**.

7
DOS TIPS AND TRICKS

Experienced users develop a collection of methods and approaches that transcend the opaque descriptions of capabilities found in the manual that accompanies DOS. Whether you call them insights or tricks, they can save a novice computer user considerable time and frustration.

Unerasing

You'd think that when you erase a file (**ERASE** or **DEL**), the file would be gone for good. If you accidentally erased the file, welcome to the cruel, harsh world.

Fortunately for those of us, nearly all of us actually, who occasionally make a mistake, deletion is not death. It is more like purgatory. When a file is deleted, it remains just where it is on the disk. The only thing that is deleted is the reference to its location kept by DOS' internal file allocation structure. If you draw a line through a table of contents reference to a chapter in a book, the chapter is still present—it is just rendered inaccessible by any means other than browsing. As long as no new information is written to the area occupied by the deleted file, the possibility of rescusitation exists.

If you have accidentally erased a valuable file, do not do anything that will write, save, or create a new file on that disk. You will not be able to retrieve a thing if new data has replaced the old. Stop, think, and if there is any chance of adding a new file in the course of further use of the system, turn off the computer or, in the case of a floppy disk, remove the disk from the drive.

Several software packages, both commercial and public-domain, will "browse" through a disk, locate a deleted file, and unerase it. A public-domain program called UNERASE is widely available from bulletin boards and copying services. A number of multi-function shareware disk utilities also will unerase files.

A great number of users have purchased one of the three leading commercial utilities packages: Norton Utilities, Mace Utilities, and PC Tools. Each includes unerase capabilities along with a wealth of other useful tools that experienced users can employ to rescue data, optimize system performance, and make life with a computer generally simpler and easier.

Unformatting

Well, if deleting files isn't necessarily synonymous with doom and dismay, certainly we should be very careful about **FORMAT** because it really does obliterate data. Right? Well, not entirely.

Mace Utilities was first to provide a means of recovering some, if not all, of the data on a drive after it has been formatted. Norton Utilities recently added the same function. Bear in mind, however, that this is a trickier proposition if you are trying to rescue data cold. Mace is batting 50 percent in retrieving material from a disk I accidentally formatted. By the time you read this, though, several new releases will have come and gone and my problems may well not be your problems.

A more certain approach is to use Mace (or a competitor) to actually format your disk in the first place. The formatting routine squirrels away additional information that is useful in performing a surer and more complete restoration of files if that should ever be necessary. To be safe from accidental reformatting, decide on an unformatting utility now, and use it religiously to format all your disks.

Getting Organized

The best way to organize a hard disk is the way that works for you. Aesthetics and personality play a large role in devising a system that suits a given individual.

Most people find it easier to work with a directory structure that is broad but not too deep. Whatever is gained in a highly hierarchical system of organization is lost in the inconvenience of specifying long pathnames to log onto a deeply buried subdirectory.

My approach is to store the bare minimum in the root directory: CONFIG.SYS and AUTOEXEC.BAT, COMMAND.COM, and a variety of temporary files that don't fit cleanly into other established niches. From the root directory there are multiple program directories and multiple data directories. Very few have their own subdirectories. The WS50 directory contains all the program files associated with WordStar Release 5.0, for instance. A PATH command in the AUTOEXEC.BAT file names WS50, along with eight or nine other subdirectories, ensuring that wherever I am in the subdirectory structure, WordStar is always "on tap" when I type **WS**.

I have a \WORK subdirectory. It contains miscellaneous files related to office activity, plus several subdirectories for specific kinds of information. \WORK\REPORTS\ holds monthly reports; \WORK\LETTERS\ contains correspondence of a general nature related to office activities. Another subdirectory is called \PROJECTS. It contains no files, just subdirectories: \PROJECTS\SCHEDULE\, \PROJECTS\NEWSLETR\, \PROJECTS\PR\, \PROJECTS\CONTRACT\, etc.

Storing data files in their own subdirectories, rather than mixing them with program files, greatly simplifies backing them up. Some folks keep data files in subdirectories within a given program subdirectory. Things can get confusing, however, if you use more than one software package to work on a given category of data.

All DOS files except COMMAND.COM are stored in the \DOS subdirectory. An extensive collection of utility programs that expand upon DOS is stored in a \UTIL subdirectory. Both \DOS and \UTIL are named in the PATH command issued whenever the computer is booted.

Disk Hygiene

Floppy and hard disks are ostensibly *permanent* storage media. The valuable programs and data that dance from chip to chip when the computer is on spend their "off" hours safely ensconced in the dizzyingly concentric magnetic universe of a disk surface.

Permanence is, in this case, fragile. Dust and dirt can physically damage a disk surface, rendering all or part of a disk unreadable. Even the particles of cigarette smoke can conceivably cause damage and data loss.

Any stray magnetic field can scramble data on the surface of a floppy disk. Keep disks away from telephones, electric pencil sharpeners, transistor radios—anything with a magnet in it. The top of a computer monitor is one of the worst places to keep disks because of the substantial magnetic and electrical fields generated by the cathode ray tube. Some components of book-theft detection systems, particularly the sensitizing/desensitizing equipment, can cause trouble. Anything with a motor or a magnet in it (e.g., speakers) could cause problems if disks are allowed to come within a few inches of it.

Beware of extreme heat and cold. The tolerances are very close in the construction of the precision read/write mechanisms used in disk drives. Motors too can be adversely affected by running at temperature extremes. The result of incorrectly functioning drives is inaccurately written data—data that may not be readable once conditions have returned to normal. Condensation caused by rapid changes of temperature can severely damage drive mechanisms. One should never attempt to run a computer that has been in low temperature conditions. Give the machine a few hours to reach room temperature, allowing it the opportunity to adjust slowly rather than all at once.

Keep in mind that the data stored on disk "ages." Stored as magnetic impulses, it can weaken gradually over time. To assure the integrity of your data you should "refresh" it every six months or every year. Just copy it from its present location to a new location. A quick way to do this on a hard drive would be to create a temporary subdirectory, copy the contents of the subdirectory to be refreshed into it, delete the original files, then copy the files back from the temporary directory.

```
MD \TEMP
COPY \OLD_DIR\*.*    \TEMP
DEL \OLD_DIR\*.*
COPY \TEMP\*.*    \OLD_DIR
DEL \TEMP\*.*
```

If you have the MOVE public-domain utility program (you really have no excuse not to get it), the routine is simpler:

```
MD \TEMP
MOVE \OLD_DIR\*.*    \TEMP
COPY \TEMP\*.*    \OLD_DIR
DEL \TEMP\*.*
```

File Fragmentation

DOS stores files sector by sector. It attempts to lay down data in adjacent sectors, as this allows for the fastest possible retrieval later on. As individual files grow in size, and as the disk as a whole fills up, however, it is not always possible to keep files contiguous. A given file may be contained in several groups of sectors scattered about the disk surfaces.

This fragmentation increases the time needed by DOS, and the computer hardware, to find and transfer into internal memory the data needed by a program. Those who imagine that their PC isn't running as fast as it was when it was first purchased may be right, and file fragmentation is the most likely culprit.

Norton Utilities and Mace Utilities are only the most widely known of a variety of unfragmenting programs available to computer users. DOG (Disk Organizer) is a widely used shareware alternative. Features, prices, and performance vary too quickly to include specific recommendations here. If you want to wring the utmost in performance from your hardware, start by investigating these products and those that claim to be equal or superior to them.

Keyboard Redefinition

Macro programs like SuperKey and ProKey offer a sophisticated means of redefining the meaning of any key or series of keys on the keyboard. They are discussed in the section on Macro programs in the "Supplementing DOS" chapter. Here we'll examine the facilities DOS itself provides for reassigning the meaning of the keys.

ANSI.SYS, the screen and keyboard device driver provided with DOS, must be installed in order to redefine keys. The following line in the CONFIG.SYS file will do the job: **DEVICE=ANSI.SYS**. Once installed, ANSI.SYS will accept "escape sequence(s)" that redefine the meaning of individual keys. Most users will find that the simplest way of sending such sequences of control characters is with the **PROMPT** command.

First, let's look at a simple example. Say we are tired of typing "etcetera." We will assign this character string to the ampersand "&" with the following **PROMPT** command:

PROMPT $e[38;"etcetera"p

From now on, whenever the user attempts to type "&," "etcetera" will be printed on the screen.

Let's dissect the command line. $e is the **PROMPT** meta-string for Escape. It and the left square bracket must precede any sequence of control characters being sent to ANSI.SYS. The next value, **38** here, is the ASCII value of the character to be redefined—the ampersand in this case. Check your

DOS manual's appendix for a list of the ASCII values of the keys on your keyboard.

Next comes a representation of the new value to be assigned to the specified key, in this case the text string "etcetera." A lowercase "p" must be the last character in the **PROMPT** command line. The user has a choice of indicating the new value as characters enclosed by quotation marks or as a series of ASCII codes, each separated from the next by a semicolon. Thus, the reassignment above could just as well have been written:

PROMPT $e[38;101;116;99;101;116;101;114;97p

To change the ampersand back to its original meaning, issue the following command:

PROMPT $e[38;38p

Any of the alphabetic and numeric keys on the keyboard can receive a new meaning using the above approach. The function keys call for a slight variation. They can only be referred to by a two-character extended ASCII value, the first character of which is always 0. Thus, to assign **DIR** <carriage return> to the F4 key, enter the following **PROMPT** command line:

PROMPT $e[0;62;"DIR";13p

Note that 13 is the ASCII value for a carriage return.

Extended ASCII codes are defined for F1 through F10, Alt-F1 through Alt-F10, Ctrl-F1 through Ctrl-F10, and Shift-F1 through Shift-F10. There are also codes for Home, PgUp, End, PgDn, Ins, Del, the arrow keys, Shift-Tab, and a number of Alt-alphabetical character combinations (consult your DOS manual).

It is relatively easy to contrive a sophisticated system of DOS commands activated by function keys, either alone or in concert with Alt, Ctrl, or Shift. Such a system would be installed whenever the system is booted through a series of **PROMPT** command lines contained in the AUTOEX-EC.BAT file. Unfortunately, using **PROMPT** to send instructions to the ANSI.SYS device driver clobbers the current DOS prompt. You should include a command line in the AUTOEXEC.BAT file, after all the reassignments have been done, that reestablishes the form of DOS prompt you would like to have.

There are no Extended ASCII values for Ctrl, Alt, Esc, Tab, PrtSc, Scroll Lock, Num Lock, and Caps Lock and thus there is no way to use **PROMPT** to reassign the meaning of these keys.

CD-ROM and DOS

CD-ROM technology is the best medium so far for putting massive amounts of data on a desktop. Unfortunately, it was not of concern when designers laid DOS' foundations in the early 1980s.

Until the advent of DOS 4.0, the operating system did not support disk storage devices larger than 32MB. So how is it that a 550-MB CD-ROM drive can be attached to PCs? The answer is subterfuge. DOS knows how to deal with block devices, like disk drives, and character devices like the screen, keyboard, and printer port. It is tricked into thinking that the drive is a character device. Since the 32-MB limit applies only to mass-storage devices, all bets on capacity are off. There are many approaches to fooling DOS into cooperation. Some have the sole effect of allowing a particular retrieval package to locate data on the CD-ROM. Others make the CD-ROM look like a huge hard disk drive. This has considerable benefits, since users are familiar with hard disks and don't need to learn any new commands.

Microsoft CD-ROM Extensions

Microsoft, originator of DOS and one of the most influential software publishers in the business, took up the task of developing a generalized means by which software could make use of the CD-ROM medium. Emulation of existing hard disk storage devices was a major priority. The result was Microsoft Extensions (MSCDEX), a program that literally extends DOS to allow it to work effectively with CD-ROM.

Any CD-ROM disc mastered according to the ISO 9660 (or High Sierra) standard will be accessible under DOS if CD-ROM Extensions are used. Universal adoption of MSCDEX should greatly simplify things for those with multiple CD-ROM products employing a variety of proprietary retrieval mechanisms.

Coping With Multiple CD-ROM Configurations

Until all publishers of CD-ROM products move to ISO 9660 and Microsoft Extensions, however, users will be in a bind. Each product may require a different environment in which to operate—its own CD-ROM device driver, BUFFERS, and FILES settings.

What is needed is a simple way to swap one system configuration for another, based on which product will be used. In practical terms, you need to store multiple CONFIG.SYS and AUTOEXEC.BAT files under something other than those two reserved filenames. On demand, the contents of the appropriate files are copied to the CONFIG.SYS and AUTOEXEC.BAT filenames and the system is rebooted immediately under the new configuration.

Copying the stored replacements to the CONFIG.SYS and AUTOEXEC.BAT filenames each time is tedious and time-consuming. A batch file routine is far better. I maintain three files for each configuration: a replacement for CONFIG.SYS with a .SYS extension, a replacement for AUTOEXEC.BAT with a .BAT extension, and a batch file to copy them to their respective filenames. To invoke the High Sierra setup I type **DOMSX**. This batch file takes care of the rest. All you need do is reboot and the new configuration will take effect. If you have access to a public-domain REBOOT program, it can be included in the batch file.

Here are the contents of the three files:

```
C>  TYPE   \UTIL\DOMSX.BAT
copy  c:\util\msx.sys  c:\config.sys
copy  c:\util\msx.bat  c:\autoexec.bat
reboot

C>  TYPE  \UTIL\MSX.BAT
path   c:\util;c:\bin;c:\dos;c:\;c:\ws4;c:\dbase;c:\dbxl
prompt  $p$_$g
timer/s
\BIN\MSCDEX.EXE  /D:MSCD000    /M:8

C>  TYPE  \UTIL\MSX.SYS
LASTDRIVE=Z
files=20
buffers=24
device=ansi.sys
DEVICE=\DEV\HITACHI.SYS  /D:MSCD000  /N:1
```

When to Upgrade to a New DOS Version

Should all users automatically upgrade to the most current version of DOS as soon as it is introduced? No. Look carefully at the enhancements provided in a new version. Only if those enhancements are important to you should you consider acquiring the new version of DOS.

If you intend to hook your computer to a local area network (LAN), DOS 3.0 or higher is required. Depending on the network operating system in use, you may indeed need the most current DOS version. It isn't uncommon to find CD-ROM products that require at least DOS 3.2. Some earlier DOS versions won't support 3 1/2" floppy disk drives, especially those capable of storing 1.44MB. If you absolutely have to have a single hard disk volume bigger than 32MB at your disposal, then DOS 4.0 or higher is for you.

Besides the cost of the new version of DOS, you should be aware of the subtleties of installation. With DOS 4.0, for instance, you cannot install the ability to handle disk volumes larger than 32MB without first repartitioning and reformatting the hard disk drive. Depending on the amount of data and programs that will have to be backed up and restored in the process, this could take several hours.

When you replace old system files with new, be sure the replacement is total. If you have multiple copies of some of the external DOS commands scattered through your subdirectories and not all of them get erased, you could run into version incompatibilities at inconvenient times.

Watch out for ".0" ("point zero") syndrome. It is axiomatic that major upgrades, usually designated by a new major version number followed by .0, contain a disproportionate number of bugs. Version x.1 usually follows quickly on the heels of x.0. If the major new features promoted by the IBM/Microsoft combine include some that you can't live without, buy but use the product cautiously until you have determined that it is solid with respect to the applications to which you will put it.

Sometimes bugs are fixed "on the fly." Later purchasers of the same version number of DOS may get program code that includes fixes to problems discovered by earlier users. The only way to catch up with such fixes is to carefully note any difficulties and complain to IBM or Microsoft (depending on whose label is involved) until their product-support people give in.

Unlike most other software products, reduced-cost upgrades from one version of DOS to the next are generally not available. If you want the new

package, you pay the same price as someone who has never purchased a copy
of DOS before. IBM broke that pattern by offering a discounted price for DOS
4.0 to users of all earlier versions of IBM-labelled DOS. Whether this is a
fluke, or the beginning of a new trend, one that Microsoft will follow as
well, is not clear as of this writing

8

SUPPLEMENTING DOS

Just because DOS provides a means of accomplishing a task doesn't mean that DOS' way is the best way. An enormous variety of utility software is available designed to manipulate files faster, with greater flexibility, or more easily than DOS allows.

Replacements for DOS Commands

DOS commands and facilities, with the exception of the DOS Shell in version 4.0, aren't fancy. They get the job done, but there are few bells and whistles that add convenience to function. Users concerned with getting the most out of their computer system, and making things as easy as possible on themselves in the bargain, should consider acquiring some of the programs discussed in this chapter to replace more primitive DOS equivalents.

Almost all these utilities are either public-domain or shareware programs. While I have spotlighted some of the programs I've found useful, you should be aware that there are doubtless numerous other programs that perform the same job. What you should get from this listing is primarily a realization of the sort of utility software that is available to improve upon DOS-provided commands, and only secondarily a line on specific packages that you should acquire. You'll find more information on public-domain software and shareware later in this chapter.

Most users will find it convenient to store these DOS substitutes in a utilities subdirectory, and make them instantly available by designating that subdirectory among others using the PATH command.

LIST.COM

SYNTAX: LIST <filespec>

PURPOSE: Views text and program files. Offers vast improvements in power and versatility over the DOS **TYPE** command.

REPLACES: TYPE

COST: Shareware price is $15.

USAGE: The following features are supported by LIST:

- page-by-page and screen-by-screen paging, forwards and backwards
- specification of multiple filenames for display one after the other, using wildcards in filenames
- search for word or words in file
- onscreen suppression of WordStar control characters, at user's choice
- split screen viewing
- optional display of data in a file in hexadecimal (of use primarily to programmers)
- easy customization of screen colors within the **LIST** display
- printing from within **LIST**

To view the documentation file LPTX.DOC, stored in the C:\UTIL subdirectory, type **LIST LPTX.DOC**. The resulting display shows the first page of the file.

| LIST | 1 | 10–19–87 12:14 | \UTIL\LPTX.DOC |

LPTx : Line Printer Output Capture Routine

Version 7.00

(C) Copyright 1987 by Mark DiVecchio, All Rights Reserved
(C) Copyright 1987 by Kepa Zubeldia, All Rights Reserved

This program is released for use in non-commercial environments. I ask commercial users to register the program with a $25 copyright fee for each site (any number of users and computers) at which the program is used.

DISCLAIMER: This program tries to perform a function which is not supported by DOS. It will work sometime and will not work other times. That kind of explains why you don't see this type of program on the market. I have tested it under DOS 2.x and 3.x. In particular, under 3.x, I used dBase-II. I have not tested it with dBase-III or dBase-III+.

Mark C. DiVecchio
10435 Mountain Glen Terrace

Command * Top of file * Options: h8kMpswTalj Keys:
X=exit ?=Help

The PgDn and PgUp keys operate as expected. Using the Enter key advances the display a screen at a time. The up and down arrows move one line at a time.

The most frequently used **LIST** commands are shown under "Options:." When they are typed, they appear next to the word "Command" at the lower left-hand corner of the screen. To find out what each does, or what commands are available from within **LIST**, press "?" or "H." The resulting help screen, rearranged here in order to fit on the printed page, is crammed with information on your options.

LIST   1   10–19–87 12:14   \UTIL\LPTX.DOC

LIST - Version 6.2a - 5/07/87
(c) Copyright 1987 Vernon D. Buerg
456 Lakeshire, Daly City, CA 94015
For personal use only. Not for sale or hire.

F1	Display HELP info	a-A	toggle APX/DV/DD
F2	change FIND bg	a-B	mark Bottom line
F3	Find next text	a-C	Clone LIST.COM
F4	change FIND fg	a-D	write to file
F5	change text bg	a-E	toggle EGA 25/43
F6	change text fg	a-F	get new Filespec
F7	change 1/25 bg	a-G	Goto DOS
F8	change 1/25 fg	a-H	toggle Hex mode
F9	Find previous text	a-J	Junk filter
F10	Exit to DOS	a-L	toggle preLoading
		a-M	Mark top line
K	toggle typeahead	a-R	toggle Ruler
P	toggle Printing	a-S	toggle Sharing
W	Wrap long lines	a-T	toggle Tabs
/	Scan for exact text	a-U	unmark lines
\	Find any case text	a-W	freeze top window

X   Exit to DOS (cls)   a-X   exit, orig screen

T HOME	go to Top of file
B END	go to Bottom of file
D PgDn	forward one page
U PgUp	back one page
c-PgUp	list previous file
c-PgDn	list next file
c-left	go to col 1
7 or 8	strip or leave hi-bit
*	star filter
+/-/#	skip to line #

If you find LIST of value,
a gift of $15, or any amount,
would be greatly appreciated.

Command   Options: h8kMpswTalj Keys: X=exit ?=Help

To view the contents of all the .DOC files in a subdirectory, you might type **LIST *.DOC**.

Ctrl-PgDn advances from the first to the second matching file; Ctrl-PgUp moves in the opposite direction.

MOVE.COM

SYNTAX: MOVE [drive:]<filespec> [drive:]<filespec>

REPLACES: COPY followed by **DEL**

PURPOSE: Quickly moves one or several files from drive to drive or directory to directory without resorting to the cumbersome process of copying files to a new location, followed by deleting them at the old location.

COST: Public domain.

USAGE: To move all the .DOC files from drive A: to drive B:, enter **MOVE A:*.DOC B:**. In reorganizing your hard disk drive, you decide to move all the .COM and .EXE files in the root directory to a \DOS subdirectory.

```
MOVE  C:\*.EXE  C:\DOS
MOVE  C:\*.COM  C:\DOS
```

In general, **MOVE** follows the syntax of **COPY**. Unlike **COPY**, however, **MOVE** will not allow you to overwrite an existing file with an incoming file of the same name.

MOVE only copies and deletes when it is moving data from one drive to another. If the move is among subdirectories on the same disk, it simply makes changes in DOS' internal bookkeeping such that the files immediately become part of a new subdirectory. Moves between subdirectories, therefore, are extremely fast.

SDIR.COM

SYNTAX: SDIR [drive:][filespec] [/X l /D l /S]

REPLACES: DIR

PURPOSE: Displays a listing of files in order by filename, extension, date, or size. Allows the user to scroll backwards and forwards through the listing without having to reissue the directory command.

SWITCHES: **/X** Display in order by filename extension.
             /D Display in order by file creation date.
             /S Display in order by file size.

COST: Public domain.

USAGE: Display in order by filename is the default. Files are shown in two columns, with file size and creation date and time provided. The full range of wildcards is available with **SDIR**. After viewing the file listing, you must press Esc to get back to the DOS prompt.

To list the contents of the \BOOK subdirectory, type **SDIR** C:\BOOK*.*. The result is the display on the following page. Note that files are listed by filename.

```
SDIR Ver 5.0                  Vol:                      18Sep88 09:56
    Directory of C:\BOOK


.                 <DIR>   20Jan88 20:30   NEXTBOOK         7936 20Apr88
21:15
..                <DIR>   20Jan88 20:30   SUPP      .BAK   9088 18Sep88
09:28
ADDL    .DOS      2176 18Sep88 00:04     SUPP      .DOS   9728 18Sep88
09:53
APPENDIX.DOS       384 10Sep88 11:01     TEXT             4104 18Sep88
08:43
BATCH   .DOS      1408 18Sep88 00:06     TEXT2            2052 18Sep88
09:54
CONTENTS.DOS      3200 17Sep88 10:45     TEXT3               0 18Sep88
09:56
ESSEN   .DOS     42240 17Sep88 22:26     TEXT9     .COM   8191 07May87
06:20
GLOSS   .DOS     18688 17Sep88 22:08     TEXTK               0 18Sep88
09:53
INDEX   .DOS       256 10Sep88 11:01     TIPS      .DOS   9088 18Sep88
00:09
INTRO   .DOS      9344 17Sep88 10:48     USEFUL    .DOS  28032 17Sep88
22:48
MASTER  .DOS       256 10Sep88 11:00

       156171 Bytes in          21 File(s);      3467264 bytes free.
```

To view just the files with a .DOS extension, and in order by size, enter:

SDIR C:\BOOK*.DOS /S

This results in the following display:

```
SDIR Ver 5.0                  Vol:                      18Sep88 09:59
    Directory of C:\BOOK

MASTER  .DOS       256 10Sep88 11:00     TIPS      .DOS   9088 18Sep88
00:09
INDEX   .DOS       256 10Sep88 11:01     INTRO     .DOS   9344 17Sep88
10:48
APPENDIX.DOS       384 10Sep88 11:01     SUPP      .DOS   9728 18Sep88
09:53
BATCH   .DOS      1408 18Sep88 00:06     GLOSS     .DOS  18688 17Sep88
22:08
ADDL    .DOS      2176 18Sep88 00:04     USEFUL    .DOS  28032 17Sep88
22:48
CONTENTS.DOS      3200 17Sep88 10:45     ESSEN     .DOS  42240 17Sep88
22:26
       124800 Bytes in          12 File(s);      3463168 bytes free.
```

NOTES: There are numerous improved versions of the DIR command available in the public domain. **SDIR** is the one I like, but you may well find an alternative that is superior in versatility, compactness, or features.

| WHEREIS.COM |

SYNTAX: WHEREIS <filespec>

REPLACES: (No DOS equivalent)

PURPOSE: Searches through all subdirectories for files matching the file specification supplied. It lists the files it finds.

COST: Public domain.

USAGE: One of the most annoying byproducts of the huge capacity of hard disk drives is the ease with which you can lose track of a file. Perhaps you inadvertently saved a text file in something other than the subdirectory you had intended. DOS provides only the DIR command. Retyping DIR and a subdirectory command for every subdirectory on the hard drive is a pretty tedious means of finding the wayward file, however. **WHEREIS** scans all subdirectories and displays all filenames that match the file specification, along with the directory path indicating where they are stored. Wildcards are okay, allowing you to find in one step files with similar but not identical names.

To locate files beginning with "LIST," assuming **WHEREIS** is either in the current directory or in a directory named in a prior PATH command, enter:

WHEREIS LIST.*
\UTIL\LIST.COM
\PFSPUB\LIST.PUB
\BOOK\LIST.COM

NOTES: WHEREIS is just one of several file-find utilities, both public-domain and commercial. **WHEREIS**, at least the version I have, is distinguished by an extremely small file size. At 512 bytes, there is always room for **WHEREIS.COM**.

| LF.COM |

SYNTAX: LF [drive:][filespec]

REPLACES: DIR

PURPOSE: Displays files grouped by their filename extensions.

COST: Public domain.

USAGE: **LF**, for List File I suppose, is an extremely simple utility that can be very useful at times. The format in which it displays files makes it helpful when you are working with a disk or a subdirectory with a large number of files. Listed by subdirectory, the files you are looking for jump out at you.

Unfortunately, **LF** doesn't accept a path as part of the file specification. You must be logged onto a subdirectory before you can use **LF** with it. Despite this considerable limitation, I still like **LF** and use it from time to time.

To display the contents of the \OVERDUES subdirectory, I enter:

CD \OVERDUES
LF

The file display provided, compressed here, looks like this:

```
.DBF files:  borrower items     itemtemp nadbill   nadfirst
             scratch  scrcall   scrshelf temp      tempborr
.FRM files:  cardlist leon      odbill   odborr1   odborr2
             odfinal  odfirst   odregis1 odregis2  odregis3
             scrshelf
.HIS files:  dbxl
.LBL files:  gail     lbl       odfbcard odfblbls  wheel
.MEM files:  odparams
.NDX files:  borrcard borrlast  borrnum  borrtown  iauthor
             icallno  iduedate  ititle   itslip    scrcall
             tempname
.PRG files:  blindtst bopaging  borrfrom borrinit  itemfrom
             odbackup odbilla   odbillb  odclear   odcustom
             odcutb   odedit    odentry  oderror   odfbconf
             odfinla  odfinlb   odflip   odflipe   odfrsta
             odjunk   odlabels  odmisc   odprint   odprod
             odquick  odreindx  odreport odscrtch  odsetup
```

To show only files beginning with "OD," I enter:

CD \OVERDUES
LF OD*.*

Resulting in:

```
.FRM files: odbill     odborr1   odborr2   odcutoff   odfinal
            odregis1   odregis2  odregis3  odshelf
.LBL files: odfbcard   odfblbls
.MEM files: odparams
.PRG files: odask      odbackup  odbilla   odbillb    odclear
            odcuta     odcutb    odedit    odentry    oderror
            odfblbls   odfinla   odfinlb   odflip     odflipe
            odfrstb    odjunk    odlabels  odmisc     odprint
            odpurge    odquick   odreindx  odreport   odscrtch
```

FINDUPE.COM

SYNTAX: FINDUPE

REPLACES: (No DOS equivalent)

PURPOSE: Lists files in different subdirectories that have the same filenames, assisting users in eliminating unnecessary duplications of files.

COST: Public domain.

USAGE: When you type **FINDUPE**, you are asked whether you want a
list of all files on the disk, one in alphabetical order by filename, or just a list
of the duplicate filenames. You can opt to send the list to the printer rather
than the screen. If the list goes to the screen, the it is displayed one screenful
at a time. Running the **FINDUPE** program so as to list only duplicate filenames produces the following display.

```
    Directory List Program  Version 1.0

    Written by
        Karson W. Morrison
        Feb. 13, 1985

    OPTIONS:
        List the entire directory of the disk: (1)
        List only Duplicate files on the disk: (2)

    Option: 2
Reading the Directories. . . . . . . . . . . . . . . . . . . . .
Sorting the Directory Data
    For output on printer enter (P) prior to number option
```

Here is the first page of a long list of duplicate filenames on my hard disk drive.

Directory list for duplicate files. 18-Sep-1988 10:49:56 am
* = Sub Dir: R = Read only; H = Hidden: S = System Page 1

Files	Date	Time	Directory
ARC.EXE	5/10/88	21:17	\DBXL
ARC.EXE	2/13/86	10:23	\UTIL
AUTO.BAT	2/ 4/88	20:51	\AUTOMENU
AUTO.BAT	2/ 4/88	20:51	\DOS
AUTOTEMP.BAT	8/ 7/88	19:12	\
AUTOTEMP.BAT	9/18/88	7:16	\AUTOMENU
* BOX	11/20/87	22:26	\
BOX	8/18/88	17:00	\WS5
BUILDWIN.EXE	1/18/88	12:00	\DBXL
BUILDWIN.EXE	3/ 1/88	17:00	\QUICK
CHECKCOM.BIN	1/18/88	12:00	\DBXL
CHECKCOM.BIN	3/ 1/88	17:00	\QUICK

More

NOTES: There are many public-domain programs that perform this function. You might look for one that displays file size along with the other information shown above. Occasionally date alone can be misleading in determining which of several files does what.

FREE.COM

SYNTAX: FREE [drive:]

REPLACES: CHKDSK

PURPOSE: Quickly reports the amount of free space on a disk drive.

COST: Public domain.

USAGE: To find out the free space on drives A: and C:, enter:

```
C:\> FREE C:
Drive C: 3438592 bytes free
C:\> FREE A:
Drive A: 238592 bytes free
```

Before installing a new software package, or copying files from one drive to another, it is frequently necessary to confirm that there is sufficient space on the destination drive to hold the new material.

CHKDSK will do the job, but it is necessarily slow given the diagnostic function it performs while it tallies up disk space. **DIR** only shows the amount of space used by existing files. Some quick subtractions, disk capacity minus the space taken up by existing files, will give you the result you're looking for, but not as conveniently as **FREE**.

TREED.COM

SYNTAX: TREED [drive:]

REPLACES: TREE

PURPOSE: Displays graphically the structure of the subdirectories existing on a given disk drive.

COST: Public domain.

USAGE: The following invocation of **TREED** produces a readily understood display of the tree-like structure of directories on a hard disk.

```
TREED C:

-+-3D
 |-ASKSAM4
 |-AST
 |-AUTOMENU
 |-BANK
 |-BANNER
 |-BIN
 |-BOOK
 |-BOX
 |-CHESS
 |-COPTER
```

```
|-DBXL——-|-TOOLS
|      |-UTILS
|-DEV
|-DOS
|-FINANCES
|-FOX
|-FRENCH
|-GENIFER—|-BIBDIR
|      |-TEST
|-GERMAN
|-HOMEBASE
|-INMAGIC
|-KIDS
|-LETTERS
|-LIB
|-LQ
|-MISC
|-NORTON
|-OD2
|-OPAC
|-PAINT
|-PFSPUB
|-PICTURE
|-PROPLUS
|-QB4
|-QUICK——|-DEMOS
|      |-UTILS
|      |-WEDIT
|-RQ
|-SC2
|-SPANISH
|-SUPERKEY
|-TRAINS
|-UTIL
|-WLB
|-WORK
|-WP
|-WS5
|-ZOO
```

You will have to use Ctrl-S to pause the display if, like the one above, it fills more than a single screen.

Still River Shell

SYNTAX: SR [subdirectory name]

REPLACES: DOS Shell, for users of DOS 4.0 or higher; for users of earlier versions of DOS: **COPY, XCOPY, DEL, TREE, TYPE, DIR, ATTRIB, MOVE** (non-DOS alternative above), **WHEREIS**(non-DOS alternative above).

PURPOSE: Makes management of disk files easier by providing a menu-based interface to the most common commands for manipulating such files.

COST: See licensing information, listed in the following pages.

```
>ADDL    .DOS<      4480  10-11-88  07:08p! Still River Shell  2.36
 APPENDIX.DOS       1664  10-11-88  07:00p!
 BACK    .BAT A       30  10-08-88  02:00p! Drive - C:
 BATCH   .DOS      28160  10-11-88  08:56p!
 CONTENTS.BAK A     3840  10-16-88  09:20a!    3162316B   (bytes allocated)
 CONTENTS.DOS A     4224  10-16-88  11:14a!     978944   (bytes free)
 ECOMMAND.BAK A    27776  10-15-88  09:10p!         96   (% allocated)
 ECOMMAND.DOS A    27776  10-15-88  09:21p!
 ECONCEPT.BAK A    31488  10-15-88  08:56p!
 ECONCEPT.DOS A    31360  10-15-88  09:01p! Directory - \BOOK\
 GLOSS   .DOS      20352  10-11-88  08:51p!
 INDEX   .DOS        256  10-11-88  08:52p!
 INTRO   .BAK      10240  10-11-88  09:10p! Set - C:\BOOK\*.*
 INTRO   .DOS A    10496  10-15-88  08:43p!
 JUNK    .BAT A      128  10-15-88  02:35p!
 JUNK2               636  09-26-88  10:26p!         35   (files)
 LIST    .COM       8191  05-07-87  06:20a!          0   (directories)
 MASTER  .DOS        384  09-26-88  10:27p!     643072   (bytes allocated)
 NEXTBOOK           7936  04-20-88  09:15p!         94   (% used)
 SHELL   .BAK A    33024  10-16-88  11:02a!
 SHELL   .DOS A    33024  10-16-88  11:10a! Free memory - 427K
===========================================================================
>Copy< Delete  Find  List  Move  Other  Prv  Sort  taG  Tree  View  Xdos [Fn]

copy file(s)                                                <ESC> to exit
```

Figure 33. The main Still River Shell Screen.

USAGE: The Still River Shell performs most of the same functions as the File System in the DOS Shell that comes with version 4.0 of DOS. It is not as polished in some respects, and it doesn't have all the nice menu-building features (though you can access prewritten batch files with the function keys), but it is a more compact and less intrusive means of enhancing file management. About the only major lack, as far as I'm concerned, is its inability to show two subdirectories on the same screen.

Here are the legal specifics regarding licensing of the Still River Shell:

Bearer License

You may evaluate, copy, or distribute this program as well as its disk-based documentation provided you make no change to them. You may charge a fee for media and handling ($9 max) but may accept no other consideration.

Evaluation Terms

You are welcome to evaluate the Still River Shell on the condition that, if you become a regular shell user, you will also register and become a supporter too.

Bill   White
P.O.   Box   57
Still   River,   MA   01467
(617)   456–3699   (VISA   or   MC)

Thank   you   for   your   support!

Registration and Updates

When you honor your $39 user fee, you will receive the Still River Shell and its printed, bound manual (160 pp., 5.5 x 8), which greatly increases the value of the program, and discounts on future orders.

Registration (manual, disk, and future m&d update)_____ $59
Registration (manual and disk) _____ $39
Registration (disk only) _____ $25
COD or PO or not US/Canada: add $8

Site License

The site license includes unlimited use of copies of the software and printed manual at the licensed site. Corporate and institutional users employing multiple copies of the shell must obtain a site license_____ $390

If you don't have DOS 4.0, Still River Shell is an excellent, low-cost alternative to 4.0's File System.

Bags of Tricks

Peter Norton was the first to create a widely used collection of utilities that performed tasks that should have been included in DOS but weren't. The Norton Utilities include facilities for unerasing files, displaying and editing the contents of program files, testing the performance of a computer system, and other useful tasks.

Paul Mace countered with the MACE Utilities. Unfragmenting and unformatting routines are the highlights of his popular product. PC Tools has achieved considerable success recently as well.

Things change rapidly in this highly competitive category of products. If you'd like to have your own arsenal of file-rescue and performance-optimizing utilities at hand, consult the most knowledgeable "techie" you can find. The discounted price ($50 to $100 generally) of one of these packages is low enough to justify even your using it only once or twice.

Macros

A macro is one, a handful, or a larger number of keystrokes saved for repeated use. Lotus 1–2–3 popularized macros. WordPerfect supports macros. Telecommunication programs often employ macros for logging onto a remote computer system. Some folks insist on calling short routines written in dBase programming syntax "macros," though they are not—at least not in the same sense.

Macros, in whatever incarnation we choose to view them, exist to save the user's time. By recording a series of commands once, often automatically in "tape recorder mode," the user is spared having to ever again type the same string of commands. A macro facility can indeed make the use of a spreadsheet, telecommunications, or word-processing program easier. At the DOS level, however, there are many ways that macros could also be used profitably. ProKey was the first widely used stand-alone macro program. Borland's SuperKey has achieved considerable popularity as well. Each allows the user to create extensive systems of automatically executing commands initiated by just a keystroke or two.

Given the menu-building facilities of the DOS Shell, the shareware program Auto-Menu and its imitators, and the wide availability of macro facilities in many popular applications programs, the need for a stand-alone macro package has diminished. If the built-in facilities fall short, however, keep in mind that the stand-alone programs may have something more to offer.

GLOSSARY

■ Application Software

Software designed for end-users, e.g., word processing, database management, as distinguished from the system software that comprises DOS.

■ Ashton-Tate Corporation

Publisher of the best-selling dBase series of database-management programs.

■ AUTOEXEC.BAT

A special variety of batch file, the contents of which are automatically run whenever the system is booted. DOS commands or any other executable program can be invoked from an AUTOEXEC.BAT file. Modifications to the file are often a part of the installation process for new software. (See the "Batch File" chapter for details and examples.)

■ ASCII

American Standard Code for Information Interchange, a system for representation of alphanumeric characters, control symbols, and other entities using specified combinations of bits. Seven-bit ASCII is standardized. It allows for definition of 128 combinations of values. Eight-bit ASCII or Extended ASCII allows for definition of a total of 256 values. The last 128 are not fully standardized, with variations from manufacturer to manufacturer. The difference between Epson and IBM graphics character sets resides in eight-bit ASCII. Some peculiarities in the display and application of control characters are also due to discrepancies in this area.

■ BASIC

One of the most popular computer languages used on personal computers, it is available in numerous dialects, and in two major varieties: interpreted and compiled. Programs written in interpreted BASIC can only be executed from within the BASIC interpreter. In a sense, two programs are running simultaneously, interacting with one another: BASIC and the program written in BASIC. A BASIC compiler produces a free-standing, independently executable machine-language program.

■ Batch File

A text file consisting of DOS commands and any other executable program names. (See the "Batch File" chapter.)

■ Booting the System

The process by which the operating system files are retrieved from disk and loaded into internal memory where they reside while controlling activity within the computer system.

■ Bulletin Board System

A software package that allows a computer with a modem to automatically answer phone calls from other computers and allow the users of those computers to interact with the system. Bulletin boards allow users to leave open messages about matters of mutual interest for one another, to transfer electronic mail and to copy designated (generally public-domain) software from the "host" system to the bulletin board caller. This is downloading. Uploading, copying files in the other direction, is also generally available.

■ Byte

A coded combination of eight binary bits that represents a letter or number according to a system for data representation in computers, i.e., American Standard Code for Information
Interchange (ASCII). For most purposes, a byte and a character can be considered equivalent.

■ CD-ROM

Compact Disc—Read-Only Memory. A technology allowing the placement of up to 550MB of digital data on a disc that can be read using a personal computer and a CD-ROM drive attached to it. The physical appearance of the disc and the manufacturing process by which copies of it are created follow closely that of compact audio discs.

■ CD-ROM Extensions

Program files developed by Microsoft Corporation that add support for utilizing CD-ROM drives to the operating system. CD-ROM extensions are usually provided by CD-ROM drive manufacturers or purchased separately. Many publishers of CD-ROM products use proprietary software for accomplishing the same functions as Extensions, obviating the need for the latter.

■ CPU

The central-processing unit, that part of the computer that coordinates the activity of all other system components. The "brain" of the system. Microcomputers, by definition, use a CPU contained on a single chip, otherwise known as a microprocessor.

■ Clone

An IBM PC-compatible computer designed to mimic the original as closely as possible. While "clone" has negative connotations in some quarters, its most important meaning is that a given machine is highly compatible and, if it has features that make it superior to the genuine IBM article, they are implemented in such a way as not to damage compatibility.

■ Cold Boot

The process of booting the system commencing with turning on the power switch or (if the system has one) pushing the reset button.

■ Communications Port

See Serial Port.

■ Compiler

A program that converts a set of instructions written according to a rigorous system of semantics specific to the compiler (source code) into an stand-alone, independently executable machine-language program that can be run under DOS without the support of any other software. Compilers are available for source code written in BASIC, C, Ada, COBOL, dBase and numerous other languages.

■ Concatenate

Combine two text strings into one. The result of concatenating "BIG" and "TIME" is "BIGTIME."

■ CONFIG.SYS

A disk file containing configuration information. When the system is booted, DOS looks for a CONFIG.SYS. If it finds one, the instructions contained in it are executed before control is passed to the user.

■ Console

The computer keyboard and monitor. CON: is the device name associated with the console.

■ Database Management System (DBMS)

A software package that provides facilities for creation and use of one or more files of interrelated information. Bibliographies, mailing lists, and inventory lists are a few examples of the kinds of things that can be treated as a database.

■ dBase
A popular database-management package that includes a powerful programming language. A number of firms sell clones of Ashton-Tate's highly popular program.

■ Default Drive
The disk drive that DOS will use in conjunction with commands that work with disks. The default drive can always be overridden by explicitly designating another disk drive. DOS always assumes a default disk drive, except when a disk error results in a DOS request for specification of a new default drive.

■ Device Driver
A program that provides DOS or an applications program with the means to work with a device that is not normally supported. Among the device drivers included with DOS are ANSI.SYS, a driver that allows a program using it to perform more elaborate tricks with the display screen than would otherwise be possible, and VDISK.SYS, a driver that allows DOS to treat part of system memory as an virtual disk drive. Many applications programs come with drivers that allow them to fully utilize the capabilities of a given printer or video display.

■ Directory
Directory has two meanings. DIR produces a directory, that is a list, of the files on a disk drive. Directory is also used synonymously with subdirectory to refer to logical subdivisions of a disk-storage device. Thus you can do a directory of a directory.

■ DOS
The disk operating system, a collection of programs that manages the interaction between a particular computer system and an applications program (e.g., spreadsheet, word processor, etc.).

■ DOS Prompt
The onscreen indication that DOS is ready to accept a command from the keyboard. If drive A: is the current default drive, the prompt may be "A>." If C: is the default drive, then "C>" may be the DOS prompt. The **PROMPT** command allows the user to change the DOS prompt to something other than the default format.

■ Drive Designator
The letter representing the drive being referred to, followed by a colon.

■ **Driver**
See Device Driver.

■ **EISA**
Enhanced Industry-Standard Architecture, a specification for an improved standard for connecting high-performance computers and their interface cards and peripheral devices. It was proposed by a group of rival manufacturers as a less proprietary alternative to IBM's Micro Channel Architecture.

■ **Editor**
A program that allows a person to enter and edit text on a computer screen and save the result to disk. The absence of printer formatting features distinguishes editors from word-processing software. Editors are generally used by programmers and others in need of a fast, compact means of creating text without any concern for printing it on paper.

■ **Electronic Disk**
A portion of random-access memory used to imitate a floppy or hard disk drive. RAM utilized in this fashion is unavailable for use by other programs. Given the heavy RAM requirements of much of the new software, electronic disks are often set up using expanded or extended memory. DOS includes VDISK.SYS, a driver that creates an electronic disk. Numerous proprietary electronic disk programs are available as well.

■ **Electronic Spreadsheet**
A category of computer program designed to emulate the accountant's oversized paper spreadsheet. Financial and statistical values can be inserted in any one of hundreds or thousands of "cells" arranged in a matrix of rows and columns. Formulas can be defined specifying the relationship of values in various cells to those in other cells. As the values contained in cells are changed, the values derived from formulas related to the changed cells also change.

■ **Expanded Memory**
Random-access memory in excess of the 640K normally addressable by DOS, conforming to the Lotus-Intel-Microsoft (LIM) expanded-memory specification. Only programs written to that specification can make use of this extra memory space. Watch out for differing, incompatible versions of expanded-memory products. Buy only the most current version.

■ **Expansion Slots**
Most PC-compatibles include slots to accommodate add-in circuit boards. Such boards provide capabilities above and beyond what is included on the

main circuit board. The circuitry to drive a video display is often added as an expansion card. Extra memory, additional ports for printer or communications output, a mouse interface, and a mainframe terminal emulation facility are just a few examples of the types of cards you might wish to add to an expansion slot. IBM PC/XT-compatible slots will accommodate only boards designed for them. IBM PC/AT-compatible slots will take both XT-compatible boards and boards developed to take full advantage of the enhanced facilities of the AT. The Micro Channel Architecture is a new standard for expansion slots incompatible with the earlier system. Only newly developed boards can be used in a computer equipped with solely a Micro Channel bus.

■ Extended Memory
Random-access memory in excess of the 640K normally addressable by DOS, imitating the IBM specification introduced by IBM with the IBM PC/AT. Only programs specifically written to take advantage of extended memory can take advantage of it.

■ Filename
The name assigned to a program or data file. DOS allows filenames to contain up to eight characters, optionally followed by a filename extension consisting of a period and up to
three characters.

■ File Specification
The combination of drive designator, pathname (if any), filename, and filename extension (if any). Often abbreviated as "Filespec."

■ Gigabyte (G)
Roughly one billion bytes.

■ Internal Memory
See Random-Access Memory.

■ Interpreter
See Programming Language.

■ Kilobyte (K)
Actually 1,024 bytes, though it is often rounded off to 1,000 to accommodate those of us not fully at home with the peculiarities of binary arithmetic. So it is that a computer with 640K of internal memory actually has 655,360 bytes available (1024 * 640).

■ **LIM**
Lotus-Intel-Microsoft standard for expanded memory. *See Expanded Memory.*

■ **Language**
See Programming Language.

■ **Logging a Drive**
Making a drive the new default drive. You log onto drive C: by simply typing C: at the DOS prompt.

■ **Lotus**
One of the largest microcomputer software companies, Lotus Development Corporation created the best-selling spreadsheet program Lotus 1-2-3.

■ **Megabyte (MB)**
Roughly one million bytes.

■ **Memory-Resident Program**
See TSR.

■ **Micro Channel Architecture**
A new system for physically and electronically connecting expansion circuit boards to an IBM PS/2 computer. Incompatible with boards designed for IBM's earlier bus, Micro Channel Architecture appeared first on the Models 50, 60, and 80. *See EISA.*

■ **Microprocessor**
A central processing unit (CPU) on a single computer chip. A microcomputer is by definition a computer employing a microprocessor as its central processing unit.

■ **Microsoft**
Microsoft Corporation developed DOS and is a leading publisher of a wide variety of computer languages and applications programs.

■ **Modem**
A device that, running with a telecommunications program, allows you to connect one computer with another via phone lines. Some modems are internal, plugging into an empty slot on the motherboard of the computer. Others are external, connecting by cable to a serial interface connector on the back of the PC.

■ **Motherboard**

The main circuit board of a personal computer. The microprocessor and random-access memory usually reside on the motherboard, though additional memory and an alternate microprocessor may be present on an expansion card. A few computer designs, however, place all motherboard functions on a board that fits into an expansion slot. Such machines are said to have a "passive backplane."

■ **Mouse**

A pointing device attached to a computer that, when the user rolls it across a flat surface, moves the onscreen cursor or some other screen pointer.

■ **Object Code**

The machine-language equivalent of the source code of a program after it has been put through a compiling or interpreting process.

■ **Parallel Port**

Circuitry and a connector allow a computer to transfer data by cable, usually eight bits at a time, to an attached printer. A few products also employ the parallel port to transfer data from one computer to another, though that is more commonly accomplished using a communications port. Parallel ports are usually designated as LPT1, LPT2, depending on how many ports are provided in the computer hardware and how many can be supported by the version of DOS that is in use. Generally the maximum is two ports.The current default port can also be referred to as PRN.

■ **Pathname**

The sequence of subdirectory names designating the location of a particular file. In order to execute a program while logged onto another subdirectory, the program filename must be preceded by the full pathname, unless a **PATH** command listing pathnames to be searched has been executed.

■ **Port**

An interface to which a printer, modem, or other external device may be attached. A location to which information destined for an external device can be directed. Parallel ports transfer information eight bits at a time. Serial ports move it one bit at a time. Printers are usually attached to a parallel port. External modems, mice (mouses?), and some inexpensive pseudo-Local-Area Networks are attached to the serial port.

■ **Printer Port**
See Parallel Port.

■ Printer Spooler

A printer utility program that helps overcome the delay in regaining control of the computer after initiation of printing. Data is sent at top speed to an area of random-access memory set aside for the purpose. As soon as the transfer is complete, the computer can be used for other things. Meanwhile, the spooler program parcels out the data at the rate the printer requires.

■ Programming Language

A program that itself provides facilities for the creation of other programs. These facilities include a command vocabulary, rules of syntax, and support for execution of the collection of commands created by the programmer. Many versions of various languages (there are usually multiple versions available from different publishers) provide a compiler, a piece of software that turns the programmer's source code into a machine-language program that can be run independent of the language itself. Other languages, most notably the BASIC often provided with DOS, feature an interpreter. The interpreter translates source code line by line every time a program is run. Thus, programs written in interpreted BASIC can only be run from within the BASIC interpreter.

■ RAM

See Random-Access Memory.

■ RAM Disk

See Electronic Disk.

■ Random-Access Memory (RAM)

The random-access, electronic memory within a computer in which programs and data reside while it is operating. It takes the form of chips plugged into the circuitry of the system. RAM comes in various capacities from 64 kilobits to 1 megabit per chip. Usually, nine chips are required to store a byte, i.e., an alphanumeric character. Most DOS computers are limited to directly addressing 640K of RAM, though additional memory configured according to expanded or extended memory specifications may be usable by some software if present.

■ Rebooting

See Booting the System.

■ Reset

See Booting the System.

■ **Restarting**
See Booting the System.

■ **Serial Port**
A device that allows data to be transferred through a cable, one bit at a time, from the computer to some other device like an external modem or printer. A serial port should be distinguished from a parallel printer port which transfers more than one bit at a time. Serial ports are usually designated as COM1, COM2, etc. depending on how many ports are provided in the computer hardware and how many can be supported by the version of DOS that is in use. Early versions of DOS support only two ports. Most serial ports conform to the RS-232C specification, though cabling and connectors can maddeningly scramble the leads carrying the required signals.

■ **Source Code**
Lines of commands as originally written in the syntax of the programming language in use. To be distinguished from Object Code.

■ **Spooling**
See Printer Spooler.

■ **Spreadsheet**
See Electronic Spreadsheet.

■ **String**
See Text String.

■ **Subdirectory**
A logical subdivision of a disk-storage device, usually a hard disk. Subdirectories are created with the **MKDIR** (make directory) command and deleted with the **RMDIR** (remove directory) command. Only empty subdirectories can be deleted. You may log onto a subdirectory with the **CHDIR** (change directory) command.

■ **System Software**
The programs that constitute DOS are sometimes referred as system software to distinguish them from applications programs. They are designed primarily to perform functions internal to the computer system and in support of applications software.

■ **TSR**
Terminate-and-stay-resident, a category of program that remains in memory

while other programs are executing. GRAPHICS and PRINT are two DOS programs that are TSRs. Popular commercial programs like Borland's Side-Kick and Rosesoft's ProKey are also TSRs. A TSR is instantly available because it is always loaded and ready. Unfortunately, the memory space it takes up will no longer be available for other programs. Also, TSRs sometimes conflict with one another, causing confusing and unpredictable results.

■ Text String
A series of alphabetic and numeric characters. Numeric values used in doing calculations are not text strings. Program code, graphics, and other data employing other than 7-bit ASCII codes for their storage and representation cannot be part of a text string.

■ Turbo
An adjective often applied to IBM PC-compatible computers that operate faster than the original IBM model they resemble. An IBM PC/XT-compatible running at 8MHz or 10MHz is a "turbo." An IBM PC/AT-compatible running at 10MHz or faster can justifiably be called a "turbo."

■ Warm Boot
Rebooting the system using the Ctrl-Alt-Del key combination.

■ Word Processor
A computer program that allows a person to enter and edit text on a computer screen, save the text on disk, and format it so as to get the desired result when it is sent to a printer.

APPENDIX

Bibliography

The following titles explore the technicalities of DOS in greater detail than is called for here, and with better examples and a more understandable style than is found in the manuals that come with DOS.

Be sure you get an edition that covers the specifics of the version of DOS you are using. The lag time between release of a new version of DOS and publication of a new edition of one of these standbys that fully explores its features can be six months to a year.

■ Devoney, Chris. Using PC DOS. 2nd edition. Que, 1987. An inclusive 867-page guide to the details of DOS through version 3.3. It covers both introductory and highly technical matters.

■ Norton, Peter. Peter Norton's DOS Guide. Revised and expanded edition. Brady, 1987. An excellent, clearly written guide with an emphasis on the needs of beginning users.

■ Simrin, Steven. The Waite Group's MS-DOS Bible. 2nd ed. Howard Sams, 1988. Crisp, clear 522-page introduction to a wide range of topics, some introductory, others for advanced users.

Sources of Public-Domain and Shareware Software

Shareware and public-domain software can be acquired through computer-users groups, online bulletin boards and consumer services, and from commercial copying services.

The best online systems are your best bet for the latest version of your favorite utility software package. You have to balance the convenience and the instant gratification against the cost of online time. If you are paying $12 per hour ($.20 per minute) and it takes five minutes to log on, download the file, and log off again, you are getting a relative bargain at $1 for the file. If you want a large collection of files, or a single large software package, however, it could easily take an hour to download the equivalent of a single floppy disk's worth of programs. A telecommunications package that allows you to construct a macro or "script" file that automates the logon, download, and logoff processes may reduce this somewhat.

The more disks worth of files you would like to try out, the better copying services start to look. Two that I've had good luck with are:

■ PC-SIG, Inc.
1030 East Duane Ave., Suite D
Sunnyvale, CA 94086
(408) 730–9291

■ The (Public) Software Library
P.O. Box 35705
Houston, TX 77235–5705
(713) 721–5205

For those with access to a CD-ROM drive, entire public-domain/shareware libraries are available from PC-SIG and from ALDE:

■ ALDE Publishing
P.O. Box 35435
Minneapolis, MN 55435
(612) 835–5240

COMMAND INDEX

GENERAL INDEX

Meckler
11 Ferry Lane West
Westport, CT 06880
203-226-6967

The ESSENTIAL GUIDE TO THE LIBRARY IBM PC

A continuing series of practical volumes for librarians using an IBM PC for technical processing, public access, and administrative support.

ORDER FORM

Please enter my order for the following volume(s) of the ESSENTIAL GUIDE TO THE LIBRARY IBM PC:

☐ *This is a Standing Order. Send each new title beginning with volume _____ as it is published at a 10% discount.*

☐ **Volume 1:** The Hardware: Set-Up and Expansion
ISBN 0-88736-033-5 $34.95

☐ **Volume 2:** The Operating System: PC-DOS
ISBN 0-88736-034-3 $34.95

☐ **Volume 3:** Library Application Software
ISBN 0-88736-035-1 $34.95

☐ **Volume 4:** Data Communications: Going Online
ISBN 0-88736-036-X $34.95

☐ **Volume 5:** Buying and Installing Generic
Software for Library Use
ISBN 0-88736-037-8 $34.95

☐ **Volume 6:** Spreadsheets for the IBM:
A Librarian's Guide
ISBN 0-88736-047-5 $34.95

☐ **Volume 7:** Database Management Systems
ISBN 0-88736-050-5 $34.95

☐ **Volume 8:** Library Applications of
Optical Disk and CD-ROM Technology
ISBN 0-88736-052-1 $34.95

☐ **Volume 9:** The OCLC Workstation
ISBN 0-88736-083-1 $34.95

☐ **Volume 10:** Shareware for Library Applications
ISBN 0-88736-184-6 $34.95

☐ **Volume 11:** Acquisitions Systems for Libraries
ISBN 0-88736-185-4 $34.95

☐ **Volume 12:** Serials Control Systems for Libraries
ISBN 0-88736-186-2 $34.95

☐ **Volume 13:** Integrated Library Systems
ISBN 0-88736-188-9 $34.95

☐ **Volume 14:** The Operating System: PC-DOS
ISBN 0-88736-350-4 $34.95

☐ **Volume 15:** Utility Software
ISBN 0-88736-529-9 $34.95

Series ISBN 0-88736-080-7

Name _____

Address _____ Organization _____

City _____ State _____ Zip _____

Purchase Order Number _____ Authorized Signature _____

☐ Please bill my organization   ☐ Payment enclosed (Required for personal orders)